HOT Topics

YOUTH ELECTIVES

Dating
College Prep
A Reason to Live

David C. Cook Publishing Co.
Elgin, Illinois / Weston, Ontario

Hot Topics Youth Electives: Dating, College Prep, and a Reason to Live
© 1990 David C. Cook Publishing Co.
All rights reserved. Except for the reproducible Student Sheets, which may be copied for ministry use, no part of this book may
be reproduced or used in any form without the written permission of the publisher, unless otherwise noted in the text.
Scripture quotations are from the *Holy Bible: New International Version* (NIV), © 1973, 1978, 1984 by the New York International
Bible Society. Used by permission of Zondervan Bible Publishers.
Published by David C. Cook Publishing Co.
850 N. Grove Ave., Elgin, IL 60120
Cable address: DCCOOK
Designed by Randy Maid
Illustrated by John Duckworth and Randy Maid
Photo by Bill Bilsley
Printed in U.S.A.
ISBN: 1-55513-204-9

CONTENTS

What's So Hot about Hot Topics?

Let's face it: You want the kids in your youth group or Sunday School class to *like* you. Sure, you want to be respected, but you want to be liked, too—at least a little.

That's why you cringe when you're called upon to teach or lead a session on a topic you know your kids will hate—say, Sibbecai the Hushathite in I Chronicles. You know you'll have to dress up that topic with funny hats, run relay races around it, and serve banana splits afterward just to keep kids from using that dreaded word—*boring*—about you.

It doesn't seem fair, does it? You do all that work, and kids turn up their noses just because they can't instantly relate to the topic.

You deserve a break. That's why we created Hot Topics Youth Electives.

Hot Sessions

First, we picked the subjects most kids are already concerned about—things like money, dating, drugs and alcohol, and careers. That's so you can announce, "Hey, kids—next week we're going to talk about money!" Sounds better than Sibbecai the Hushathite any day, doesn't it?

Then we got some of the country's most experienced writers of youth programming to come up with sessions that explore those hot topics. We gave those writers a challenge: to create sessions that were full of creative activities *and* substantial Bible content. Each session would have to be usable in Sunday School *and* youth group, aimed at high schoolers but adaptable to junior high. Preparation would have to be easy, too—no forcing the leader to collect 300 bottle caps, two films, and an armadillo to do the session.

It was a tall order, but they did it.

Hot Tips

Next we contacted some of the most respected youth workers and speakers around—people like Josh McDowell, Jim Burns, and Barry St. Clair. We asked them to tell you how to approach these hot topics with your kids. We told them to think of themselves as friendly advisors sitting across the kitchen table from you. The resulting how-to articles would help you get ready for each unit of sessions.

That was a tall order, too—but they came through with flying colors.

Hot Format

There was still one thing left to do. We had to make sure each book was easy to follow. So we clearly marked each session's aim, key verses, and materials at the start (we called them The Point, The Passages, and The Preparation). We gave every step in the session a title and goal of its own. We put instructions to you in regular type, things you might say to kids in bold type, and suggested answers in parentheses.

We also put reproducible student sheets at the end of each unit of sessions. That's so you don't have to buy separate student books or worksheets.

Have It Your Way!

These sessions aren't just hot. They're flexible. They're active enough for youth group meetings and retreats, biblical enough for Sunday School. You can use this book in all sorts of ways. For instance:

• Use it for a 13-week quarter, leading the 12 regular sessions and one of the bonus sessions.

• Use it for a month at a time, working your way through a topic for four or five weeks.

• Use single sessions whenever you need them.

In other words, you can use them any time you want to get kids talking about—and applying biblical principles to—their favorite subjects.

Do that, and you may become one of their favorite leaders. And next time you have to talk about Sibbecai the Hushathite, they may even listen.

Have a hot time with these topics!

—*John Duckworth, Editor*

How to Talk to Kids about Dating

by Josh McDowell

Just mention the word *dating* and you have everyone's attention. It seems that everyone who is eligible to date is either waiting to, wanting to, or actually dating.

There are unique problems at each level of dating. For those waiting, they will never be old enough. For those wanting, the phone will never ring—and if it does it will be the wrong person. For those actually dating, it's hard to think about anything beyond what is happening Friday night.

We as adults tend to treat young people's problems too lightly. I've found that young people take their problems just as seriously as you or I take ours. They want to know what to expect from love, sex, and dating.

We need to give kids a lot more information, and at an earlier age, than used to be necessary. If we are going to shape what young people think about sexuality and dating rather than letting the secular culture shape it, we have to start teaching them before the values of society begin to mold their understanding.

God and Dating

Though the Bible doesn't refer specifically to dating, it does contain clear direction on relationships. As you teach God's Word, you will help your youth discover the differences between the styles of dating they normally see at school—and God's style of dating.

God loves them and has their best interests at heart—from their home lives to their school lives to their dating lives. Because He loves them, Jesus Christ wants to be in the center of dating relationships. God desires to be the focal point of every aspect of kids' lives—including dating.

This may surprise many of your teens. In fact, it may shock them to realize that God cares as much about their dates as they do!

Preparing to Teach

Modeling relationships, not dogma, affects teens' lives. Many youth workers fall into the trap of thinking that if they tell their youth groups often enough or creatively enough what the Bible teaches about relationships, the truth will eventually sink in and become part of the young people's actions.

On the contrary, the most effective strategy a youth worker can use is to be a positive model for his or her teens. The testimony of your lifestyle will serve to underscore the biblical truths you teach.

Young people are crying out for relationships that work. The greatest thing a married youth worker can do for a youth group is to love the members of his or her family, spending time to communicate with them. If you are single you can have the same effect by modeling positive relationships with your friends and the people you choose to date.

Your relationship with the Lord affects teens' lives. Your life is the greatest weapon you can use in fighting for the hearts of the young. I Timothy 1:5 says, "The goal of this command is love from a pure heart and a good conscience and a sincere faith." A pure heart results from refusing to be caught up in materialism, success, and other worldly pursuits. A good conscience results from having no ill relationships with any other person. A sincere faith results from putting into practice the knowledge you have already obtained.

Teens have a keen sense for seeing through hypocrisy. According to one youth worker, "Kids just want to see your heart. They see through all the little false impressions you put on to where your heart really is." If you want teens to apply your instruction on dating, be honest with them and with yourself.

Tips on Talking

Here are five suggestions to consider as you talk to kids about dating:

Be innovative. Reaching today's teenagers requires innovation—an ability to adapt to how they think and what they value. While the message remains the same, its presentation should be the kind kids can relate to. At times I, too, have changed my presentation to meet the needs of a particular group.

Be personal. Because we live in such a fragmented society, such a technological culture, people are not feeling close to others. Young people want to know the person who is speaking to them. I find it is most effective to relate biblical truths through recounting personal experiences.

Be transparent. Be transparent (with discretion) about your own struggles with temptation that arise in relationships. This will create an atmosphere in which young people can identify with you, learn from your mistakes, and see the Lord work through your life.

Remember that kids are in transition. Depending on the age range of the group you are leading, you will find various stages of maturity and experience. Try to remember that these young people are stuck somewhere between childhood and adulthood, innocence and experience.

Many will still want to be told answers to questions like, "What am I supposed to do? How am I supposed to act?" Others will think they already know everything and are able to make decisions for themselves. Try to strike a balance in your message. Prepare kids to deal with the downside of the big three—puberty, passion, and peer pressure—regardless of where they find themselves on the continuum of knowledge and experience.

It is especially important when leading these sessions on dating to remember that your young people are not immune to sexual involvement simply because they are actively participating in Bible study and church activities. Our "Why Wait?" teen survey of evangelical youth clearly showed that by the age of 18, 65% have been involved in varying degrees of sexual intimacy.

Provide hope. While you are teaching God's standards for relationships, you will want to provide hope for those who have already "blown it." I have found that young people in need of forgiveness require special attention.

People with sexual guilt may have serious difficulties with the concept of forgiveness. For example, some have problems believing that God can or will forgive them. Others are either unable or unwilling to accept His forgiveness. And few can forgive themselves. As a result there are many youthful Christians who have asked for God's forgiveness—and are forgiven—who go through life without experiencing the benefits of that forgiveness.

I believe that whatever help or guidance we provide in the area of dating must be in the context of loving relationships. It is especially important as youth leaders not just to talk about God's standards, but also to emphasize how to get back into a right relationship with God once a person has "blown it."

You Can Win the Battle

There is a battle raging today for the bodies and souls of America's teenagers. Like it or not, our young people are on the front line. Guilt, loss of self-esteem, broken hearts, and breakdowns in relationships are just some of the results of dating outside the boundaries of God's standards.

Please don't conclude that the struggle to protect our young people is hopeless, however. Your willingness to lead these sessions says to your youth group, "You are important and the choices you make count."

By sharing both the positive and negative experiences of your own life you will communicate, "It is never too late to start doing what is right—but it's much easier to make these decisions right at the start of a dating relationship."

If you share your ideals about love and dating, your young people will believe there is hope, and that they *can* live within God's boundaries.

We can help our young people form good, healthy dating relationships and resist the tremendous pressures to become sexually involved before marriage. With God's help, you can win the battle.

Josh McDowell is a popular speaker and author with a special concern for young people. His many books include Teens Speak Out: What I Wish My Parents Knew about My Sexuality *and, co-authored with Dick Day,* Why Wait? *(Here's Life Publishers).*

DATING

by Larry Keefauver

Dr. Larry Keefauver serves as pastor at First Christian Church in Lubbock, Texas. His books include *Friends and Faith* and *Starting a Youth Ministry*, both published by Group Books.

Many teenagers assume dating is a necessity. When their friends start dating they often want to begin dating, too—without understanding what dating is all about for a Christian.

Is dating necessary to be happy and fulfilled as a teenager? How does being a Christian make a difference in dating? This session will help you explore with your kids the question, "Why date in the first place?"

Why Date?

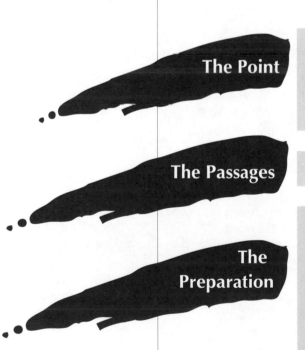

The Point

To help kids discuss their assumptions about dating; to help them decide which dating objectives are compatible with biblical principles; and to assure those who are not dating that their worth doesn't depend on whether they date.

The Passages

James 3:17, 18; Colossians 3:12-14; Matthew 5:1-10

The Preparation

You'll need:
• Two small prizes (optional)
• Bibles
• Pencils
• Copies of "Who Are You Trying to Impress?" (Student Sheet 1)
• Copies of "Christian Dating?" (Student Sheet 2)
• Chalkboard and chalk or newsprint and markers

Opening Lines
Approaching the Subject of Dating

Have kids pair up as they enter the room. When everybody's arrived, explain: **I'm going to assign you a situation in which a guy and girl are meeting for the first time. You'll have three minutes to come up with your best lines for one of you to use in introducing yourself to the other. You'll tell us your best lines by acting out the scene.**

After each skit we'll all applaud. I'll be the applause meter, keeping track of how much applause I think you've gotten. We'll see which pair can come up with the most clever, brilliant opening lines for meeting a new, prospective date.

Assign one of the following situations to each group:

1. You're a guy in the lunchroom at school. An attractive girl you've never seen before is seating herself at a table. You go over and sit down next to her. You want to meet her and ask for a date.

2. You're a girl at the mall, just walking around with your friends. You see a guy who goes to another school. He's been introduced to you before by some of your friends. He joins your group to walk around. You'd like to know him better and go out with him. What do you say?

3. You're a guy sitting with your youth group in the back row at the church worship service. You find yourself sitting next to a new girl whose family has just joined your church. How do you get to know her and ask for a date before she leaves with her family after church?

4. You're a girl. A friend of yours has met the perfect guy for you to date, or so she says. She's told him all about you and says he would really like to meet you. She has his phone number. He told her that if you'd like to go out, you should give him a call. What do you say on the phone?

Let kids have a good time with their roleplays, hamming it up as much as they want to. You don't need to discuss what should or shouldn't have been said. Just enjoy the fun—and get a feeling for how comfortable the group seems to be with the subject of dating in general. Award prizes to the winning pair if you like.

In My Opinion . . .
Revealing Assumptions about Dating

When I say the word "dating," what do you think of?

Do you think dating is a good way for people of the opposite sex to get to know each other? Is it the only way?

What do you think is the best age to start dating . . .

• In groups or on double dates?

• One person, when your parents take you to something like a school event or restaurant?

• One person without chaperones, when one of you drives the car?

If you had a date next Saturday night, where would you want to go?

Where would your parents *not* want you to go?

How late do you feel you should be able to stay out on a date?

What do your parents think?

Who pays for dates, and where does the money come from?

Do parents need to meet the person you date? Why or why not? How would you introduce the person to your parent(s)?

Do you think it's necessary to date?

If you aren't dating, but some of your friends are, would it matter to you? What might kids who are dating say about kids who aren't? (That they're still little kids, can't get a date, etc.)

Point out that Jesus and John the Baptist were single. Both had a number of friends, but apparently didn't "date" and never married. They weren't immature, and they weren't worth less for not dating.

If a person today never dated, what might he or she miss? (Romantic love, fun, marriage, etc.) **What might he or she gain?** (Time, energy, and money for other things; getting to know people of the opposite sex as friends without romantic pressures.)

Be sure to point out the value of "group dating," in which several kids just go out to have fun—without romantic pressures. It can be a good way for guys and girls to meet, or simply to learn social skills. It can also minimize the temptation of sexual involvement that often accompanies one-to-one dating.

Very Impressive
Uncovering Hidden Motives for Dating

Hand out Student Sheet 1, "Who Are You Trying to Impress?" Kids who are dating should fill it out to reflect their current practices; kids who aren't dating should fill it out as if they were. After kids total their "A" responses, discuss:

Why do some kids want to impress others with the way they date? (To be accepted; so that people will think they're sexy or rich or popular, etc.)

How could dating that way hurt you or others? (You might "use" a person without regard for his or her feelings; you might concentrate so much on impressing people that you wouldn't have fun or get to know your date, etc.)

Why do some kids try so hard to find a boyfriend or girlfriend through dating? (To feel good about themselves, to be less lonely, to get sex, etc.)

How could that hurt you or others? (Feeling like a failure if you don't get a boyfriend or girlfriend; rushing into a relationship whether or not you're right for each other; "going too far" in an attempt to keep the other person.)

If you don't have a boyfriend or girlfriend, or if you don't have "impressive" dates, how could you feel better about yourself? (Trust God to provide a companion for you; remember God loves you; make friends with people who don't have friends, etc.)

If your total on the survey was more than five, maybe you're trying to impress others or yourself—instead of pleasing God—with your dating habits.

Let's find out whether there's a better way to approach dating.

What's God Got to Do with It?
Exploring Biblical Attitudes and Dating

Hand out Student Sheet 2, "Christian Dating?" Have kids, working in pairs again, fill in the left side of the sheet with 15 biblical attitudes they can find in Matthew 5:1-10, Colossians 3:12-14, and James 3;17, 18. The right side of the sheet is for kids to write a way to show each biblical attitude in dating.

Many answers are possible; don't expect your group's to exactly match the following. But offer these in addition to the ones kids find:

1. *Attitude:* Meekness (humility). *Action:* Finding out what the other person would like to do; seeing a date as a gift to the other person.

2. *Attitude:* Seeking righteousness. *Action:* Wanting to date the people God wants you to spend time with.

3. *Attitude:* Merciful. *Action:* Forgiving the other person for being late; not making sarcastic comments to others about a date you didn't like.

4. *Attitude:* Being pure in heart. *Action:* Planning to stay away from sexually tempting situations instead of hoping to "score."

5. *Attitude:* Making peace. *Action:* Talking through a disagreement instead of fighting or giving each other the silent treatment.

6. *Attitude:* Being persecuted for Jesus' sake. *Action:* Refusing to go along with sin, even if the person stops going out with you.

7. *Attitude:* Being holy, chosen by God. *Action:* Putting God's standards over your or your date's wants.

8. *Attitude:* Compassion. *Action:* Maybe dating a lonely person; when turning someone down, not being cruel.

9. *Attitude:* Kindness. *Action:* Treating the other as special; listening and caring.

10. *Attitude:* Gentleness. *Action:* Using only gentle words and touch.

11. *Attitude:* Patience. *Action:* Letting a relationship grow naturally instead of forcing it.

12. *Attitude:* Love. *Action:* Wanting what's best for the other person, even if it means letting him or her go out with someone else.

13. *Attitude:* Being considerate. *Action:* If you have to cancel a date, letting the person know as soon as possible.

14. *Attitude:* Being impartial (fair). *Action:* Keeping other qualities—not just looks—in mind when choosing a date.

15. *Attitude:* Being sincere. *Action:* Not saying "I love you" to manipulate a person, but only if you mean it.

As you go through the list, write kids' most practical suggestions on the chalkboard or newsprint. Discuss how these biblical attitudes differ from those on Student Sheet 1.

What about Me?
Rating Our Dating

Step 5

If it would help kids to concentrate, ask them to close their eyes as you make the following comments.

Think about your own feelings toward dating. As I ask these questions, pick out one that applies to you:

What do you do and talk about on a date that shows how you feel about the Lord?

Is there sin in your dating relationship that needs to be confessed—like getting too involved physically, or making sarcastic comments about your date, or fighting too much?

When on a date, do you consider only your own needs and wants, not the other person's?

Are you forgiving when your dating partner hurts your feelings?

Do you have pure motives for what you expect of your date?

Are you seeking to please God or just each other?

If you're not dating, do you feel something's wrong with you—even though God loves you whether you date or not?

Which question "touches a nerve" in you? In silence, answer that question truthfully to God. Then ask Him to show you one step to take to grow in that area this week.

Close the silent prayer time with a prayer of your own.

What comes first—a dating relationship or a personal relationship with Jesus Christ as Lord and Savior? Too often, Jesus is an afterthought instead of a forethought. A couple dates, gets romantically involved, and *then* thinks about spiritual compatibility. This session will help your kids think first about their own and a potential date's relationship with Christ before that first date.

Getting Choosy

The Point

To help kids understand the wisdom of not getting romantically involved with non-Christians; and to help them ask spiritually discerning questions before the first date.

The Passages

Genesis 24:1-4, 10-28, 48-51; I Corinthians 15:33; II Corinthians 6:14, 15; Proverbs 12:26; 16:13; Luke 5:29-32

The Preparation

You'll need the following:
• Bibles
• Newsprint and marker or chalkboard and chalk
• Copies of "Dating Tic Tac Toe" from Step 1
• Copies of "Do You Really Go Together?" (Student Sheet 3)
• Cut-apart copies of "What Happens If . . . ?" (Student Sheet 4)
• Pencils and paper

Dating Tic Tac Toe
Exploring What It Means to Be Compatible

Before the meeting, make copies of the following tic tac toe chart. (If most of the kids in your group don't date yet, make your own chart using friendship experiences such as "Told a secret to a friend, who spread it around.")

Begin the meeting by passing out the charts. Have kids wander around the room, looking for other group members who have had an experience described on the chart. When a student finds someone who has gotten sick on a date, for example, the latter person initials that box on the seeker's chart. As soon as a student has three initialed boxes in a row (in any direction), he or she can sit down.

Started the date with a bad first impression but liked my date later	Had a blind date that was a real dud	Went to an embarrassing movie
Asked to dance but didn't want to	Got sick on a date from something I ate	Discovered I'd worn the wrong kind of clothes
Had to borrow money for a date	Went on a really boring date	Found my date wasn't the good Christian I'd thought

After the group has had about five minutes to try for three in a row, have them sit down. Say something like: **Practically everyone who's dated has had an embarrassing or funny thing happen. Sometimes those things happen because the people on the date aren't compatible—they don't get along well.**

What qualities make two people really get along as dating partners? (Common interests, tastes, background, spiritual commitment, etc.)

Let's look more closely at one area of dating compatibility—the spiritual kind. Do you ever think about whether or not a person is a Christian before you go out on a date?

Are there certain things you look for that might suggest to you whether or not a "datable" person is a Christian? (Goes to church; involved in youth group; hangs around with Christians; avoids destructive things like drugs, profanity, etc.)

Nothing in Common?
Seeing the Importance of Dating Christians

Write this statement on the board or newsprint: "Not every date leads to marriage—but all marriages start with dating."

Have everyone in the group stand. Tell kids that the wall on your right represents "I agree completely." The wall on your left represents "I disagree completely." The middle of the room means "I am undecided." Ask kids to move toward the part of the room that best represents how they feel about the statement you've written. Have a spokesperson for each response summarize reasons for taking that "stand." You may want to point out that in some cultures marriages are arranged by parents or matchmakers, so those marriages don't start with dating. But most if not all marriages in western culture seem to involve dating in the early stages of courtship.

After bringing the group back together, discuss:

Do you believe Christians should marry only Christians?

If it's possible that dating can lead to marriage, should you date only Christians?

Should you date a non-Christian with the idea that he or she will change?

Let's see what biblical principles might apply to these questions.

Form two teams. Assign Team One to read Genesis 24:1-4, 10-28, 48-51. Team Two should read II Corinthians 6:14, 15; Proverbs 12:26; I Corinthians 15:33; Luke 5:29-32. Each team should paraphrase its passages to show how the story or principle might apply to dating today. For instance, a story could be retold with modern characters in a modern setting that involves dating. Principles could be rephrased in words that mean more to today's kids. After allowing time for the paraphrases, regather the whole group and discuss results. Here are some possible paraphrases:

Genesis 24:1-4, 10-28, 48-51 (updated)

Desiring a good person for his son to date, a father sent one of his employees to scout out the youth group for a fitting blind date. He went to the local watering hole—McDonald's—where the youth group was having Cokes after a meeting. The scout saw one girl, beautiful and shy, sitting off by herself. The scout sat down next to her and said, "You seem to be lonely tonight and apart from the group."

"Yes," she said. "Most of the girls in our group have boyfriends, but I haven't found one yet."

At this the scout rejoiced. He knew just the solution. "My boss told me that his son is looking for a girl of the same faith. Could I give him your name and phone number? It could be a super blind date." Shyly she responded with her number. The employee rushed back to his boss with the good news.

Principles to draw from this story: If you're going to get romantically involved, it should be only with someone who shares your faith (Abraham didn't want his son to marry a Canaanite); God cares when we have trouble finding the right kind of people to date (or marry).

II Corinthians 6:14, 15

Stay clear of dating non-Christians. You might get romantically involved before your spiritual lives are compatible. The most important common ground between partners is commitment to Jesus Christ. What compatibility is there between Christians and unbelievers where very close relationships are concerned?

Proverbs 12:26

Be careful when forming a dating friendship.

I Corinthians 15:33

Avoid dating people who could lead you astray, who encourage you to do things that are wrong (this could include some who call themselves Christians).

Luke 5:29-32

Don't avoid non-Christians completely. In groups with other Christians, associate in a positive way with non-Christians so that they will see the healing, wholesome power of Christ in your life.

The Right Choice
Helping Kids Measure Dating Choices Spiritually

Hand out copies of "Do You Really Go Together?" (Student Sheet 3) so that kids can fill it out. After they complete the sheet, ask:
Which statements were the hardest for you to agree with?
How much of the circle should be shaded for Christian dating partners to feel they're spiritually compatible?
Encourage those who are currently dating one person to discuss the survey with that person this week.

When the Time Comes
Asking Questions to Determine Compatibility

Give each person a copy of a situation you've cut from "What Happens If . . . ?" (Student Sheet 4) As you randomly deal out the four situations, your group will be divided into four smaller groups. Ask the small groups to read the situations and decide how a Christian might handle the problem.
After about five minutes, regather the whole group and share results.
As each situation is shared, discuss these questions before moving to the next situation:
Do the rest of you agree with the response?
Would that response please God?
How would you improve on the response?
Here are comments you might share as each situation is discussed, adding your own insights:
Situation 1: **You might ask some questions to get to know the person. For instance, "Would you like to go to church or to youth group with me on Sunday?" This opens up the door for your potential date to say where (or whether) he or she goes to church. Or you might ask, "Could we go to your church or youth group for our first date?" That also lets him or her know where your priorities are.**
Situation 2: **When put on the spot in front of friends, you don't have to give an answer right away. You might say, "Thanks for asking. I need to talk with you more about this and to ask my parents. Could you call me tonight at home?" When the person calls, you could ask him or her to get involved in youth group before dating.**
Situation 3: **You might invite the person to join you and your family one week at church, or to go to a youth group event.**
Situation 4: **Your romantic feelings might keep you from looking objectively at your relationship on a spiritual level. It would probably help to talk about this with your parents, pastor or youth pastor, or even a mature Christian friend. Let them help you to back off from the romantic part of the relationship and to work on the spiritual part.**

Are All the Good Ones Taken?

Trusting God to Provide Christian Companionship

Do you think it's easy or hard to follow the advice to date only Christians? Why or why not?

Write on the board or newsprint these phrases: "Good looks"; "A lot of fun"; "Great sense of humor"; "A lot in common"; "A special person."

It's often tempting to date or want to date non-Christians. Picture in your mind non-Christians you might be tempted to date. What qualities attract you to them? Just think about it. This list may help.

Now think about one or two of these qualities that attract you most. Picture in your mind Christians you know who may have some of these qualities. If you want to date, but don't want to date these Christians, what's the reason? Pride? Shyness? Not good-looking enough for you? Too serious? Are you too critical of the available Christians?

Some of you may be thinking, "I would date a Christian if I could only find one, or one that meets my expectations." Sometimes we're impatient with God. A very special person may be around the corner in our lives if we will just wait to meet him or her. Sometimes we're so impatient to have someone to date, we often reach for the most available person instead of God's best.

Write another list on the board or newsprint: "Courage to risk meeting new Christians"; "Patience"; "More trust in God"; "A desire for God's best in my life."

Which of these qualities do you need more of in order to date really compatible people?

Let kids share their responses if they wish, but don't press for answers. Close by reading the list as kids pray silently about their dating choices.

A popular cheerleader at a Colorado high school was invited out by the star football quarterback. It appeared to be a "dream date." After a couple of dates, though, she refused to accept further invitations from him. Asked by her parents what the problem was, she replied, "Our dates were dull. All he wanted to do was talk about himself."

Fortunately, there are plenty of other ways to spend time on a date. But which of them are best for Christians? Where should your kids go on dates, and what should they do when they get there?

Should your kids try to accomplish any goals in dating beyond having a good time? What makes dates fulfilling to the couple and pleasing to God?

All these questions—and others—are the subject of this session.

Now What Do We Do?

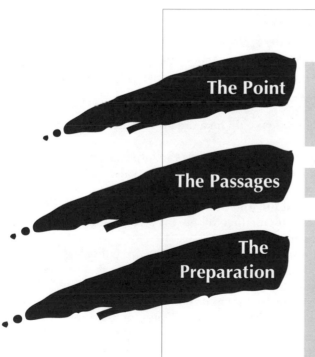

The Point	To help kids identify dating attitudes and actions which reflect obedience to God—and that help kids get to know each other socially, spiritually, mentally, and emotionally.
The Passages	Galatians 5:13-25
The Preparation	You'll need the following: • Poster board and markers • Chalkboard and chalk or newsprint and marker • Bibles • Copies of "Your Dream Date" (Student Sheet 5) • Copies of "Your Dating Circles" (Student Sheet 6) • Old phone books • Copies of entertainment sections from the newspaper • Scissors and glue • Masking tape or thumbtacks

A Dating Game
Choosing Favorite Dating Activities

Before the session, tape or tack four pieces of poster board or newsprint to the walls—or place them in various spots throughout the room. Put one of these titles on each sheet:
- "Worst Places to Go on a Date"
- "Most Embarrassing Thing That Could Happen on a Date"
- "Best Places to Go on a Date"
- "Most Boring Thing to Do on a Date"

Have plenty of markers available. As kids arrive, ask them to draw pictures or symbols on each poster that fit the poster's title—for example, a drawing of a lawnmower under "Most Boring Thing to Do on a Date." Tell kids to put their names or initials by their pictures.

When everyone's had a chance to draw, pick two teams. The object is to guess what the pictures represent. Naturally, the person who drew a picture can't be a guesser when his or her drawing is on the line. But he or she should yell, "Correct!" when the right answer is called out. If one team fails to guess in a minute or less, the second team tries. If that team fails also, then the person who drew the picture explains its meaning. The team with the most correct guesses wins.

Then have kids explain why they drew the pictures they did.

What are the best places in our town to go on a date?
What are the worst places?
Where do most of your friends go on dates?
For you, what's the difference between a great date and a disaster?

Date with a Dream
Seeing That Dating Is Fun with a Purpose

Give each person Student Sheet 5, "Your Dream Date." Give kids plenty of time to fill in their ideas of a perfect date. Then discuss the results as kids are willing.

Do you think your dream date would be a dream for the other person? Why or why not?

Would your dream date help you understand the other person better?

Where we go and what we do on a date reflects our values and what we hope will happen on a date. For example, going to a museum or art exhibit helps us learn more about the other person's way of thinking and his or her artistic tastes. Going on a picnic together might give a couple time to talk and share ideas and feelings.

Some dates help us learn more about the other person. Other dates focus our attention away from him or her. Let's list some dates that would be helpful for knowing more about the other person. Then we'll list dating situations that distract from sharing with him or her.

Go to the chalkboard or newsprint and write, "Dates for Knowing Each Other." Have kids share their ideas while you write them down. Don't comment on the ideas they give; simply list what they mention. (Examples: Meeting the person's family, cooking something together that he or she likes, etc.)

Now make a second list. Title this one, "Dates That Distract from Knowing Each Other." (Examples: Movies and sports events, watching TV, etc.—unless we spend a lot of time discussing what we've seen.)

Would you suggest moving any items from one list to the other?

Our choices of where to go and what to do on dates could affect us for a long time—even for the rest of our lives. How could each of the following dating choices affect your future?

   • **Not really getting to know the person you date.** (You could miss out on a great person; or you might make the mistake of marrying someone you had nothing in common with, or who would turn out to abuse you.)

   • **Spending a lot of time alone together in a parked car.** (Getting sexually involved, which could lead to guilt, disease, or unwanted pregnancy.)

   • **Trying to impress the other person by always going to expensive restaurants.** (Not having money to spend on anything else; attracting only people who like expensive things; marrying someone who would insist on having "the best"; always having to pretend you have more than you really do.)

When dating choices can be that important, we need all the help we can get to choose wisely. Let's see what guidelines we can find in the Bible to help us make those choices.

Watching Where You're Going
Measuring Dating Activities by Biblical Standards

Form small groups of two to five students each. Give each small group two sheets of poster board, markers, and these instructions:

At the top of one of your pieces of poster board, write, "Out of Step with the Spirit." At the top of the second write, "In Step with the Spirit." Then read Galatians 5:13-25 as a group. List on the top third of each poster the qualities you find in the passage which fit that category.

After allowing time for kids to discover and record the qualities, check their lists against this one:

Out of Step	*In Step*
Sexual immorality	Love
Impurity	Joy
Debauchery (wild partying)	Peace
Idolatry and witchcraft	Patience
Hatred	Kindness
Discord (fighting/disagreements)	Goodness
Jealousy	Faithfulness
Fits of rage	Gentleness
Selfish ambition	Self-control
Dissensions	
Factions and envy	
Drunkenness	
Orgies	

Now give small groups scissors, glue, old phone books, and copies of recent entertainment sections from local newspapers.

It's time to show what kinds of dates you think are out of step with the Holy Spirit, and which are in step—using the guidelines on your lists. Cut out ads or just names and phone numbers of places people might go on dates. Look for as much variety as you can—parks, bars, museums, restaurants, movies, miniature golf, etc. Paste these on your poster board according to whether you think such a date would be "Out of Step" or "In Step." Be ready to explain your choices.

After about ten minutes, let groups display and explain their posters. Discuss their choices with questions like these:

Which places do you feel are unwise for Christians to go on dates?
Answers will vary. Help kids to base their choices on the Galatians list. For example, going to a place that serves alcohol could lead to drunkenness; a sexually-oriented movie could lead to impurity; a violent film could encourage hatred or rage. Some activities could be unwise because of a person's attitude; even an evening of playing Monopoly could encourage discord and jealousy in an overly competitive person.

Ask kids to tell which poster they'd put the following dates on:
• **Going to an "R"-rated movie;**
• **Going to a restaurant that serves alcohol, even if you don't drink there;**
• **Going to a place that might not tempt you to sin, but might tempt the person you're dating or a "weaker" Christian who sees you going there.**
What do your posters tell you about the number of good dating options open to you? (Probably that there are plenty of things for Christians to do on dates.) Add up all the "In-Step" ideas to emphasize that wholesomeness and fun aren't opposites—no matter what our society tells us.

In Certain Circles
Evaluating Our Own Dating Habits

Give out Student Sheet 6, "Your Dating Circles." Have kids complete the sheet and discuss their answers. Explain that if the activities they listed on the outer circles also belong in the inner circle labeled "Spiritually," kids can be pretty sure those activities will meet their dating needs in a balanced way.

Christ is the unseen partner on every date. Ask yourself: Is this a place I would want Christ to see me in? Am I doing and saying what pleases Him?

If you don't plan to use the optional Step 5, close in silent prayer—giving kids an opportunity to talk to God about their dating habits and plans.

Call-ups and Turndowns (optional)
Setting up an "In-Step" Date

Once you decide what to do on a date, there's still the matter of asking the person out. Let's see what the "In Step" qualities have to do with this.
Choose a couple (guy/girl if possible). Seat the pair in front of the group.
Here's the situation: One person is calling the other with an invitation to a [fill in name of a Christian singer or band most of your kids like] **concert. What are some things the "asker" needs to tell the "askee"?**
(The day and time of the date; when the concert starts and ends; whether they'll go someplace before or after the concert; when they'll be home; how they'll get there; if by car, who's driving, etc.)
Since parents will probably want to know the things on this list, it's good to get the information the first time around. Which of the "In Step" qualities should the couple pay special attention to during this conversation?
(They're all important. For instance, if the "asker" feels God's peace, he or she won't have to panic if the conversation is a little awkward; a gentle "askee" who doesn't want to go out will reject the date, not the person.)
Have the couple act out two conversations—one in which the date is accepted, and one in which it is turned down. After each roleplay, let the group suggest improvements based on the Galatians list.

"How far can I go on a date?"

Whether or not kids ask this aloud, many wonder where to draw the sexual line when dating. Adults tell them not to go "too far," but seldom define what that means.

Teenagers' "skin hunger," curiosity about sex, and deep need for intimacy often lead them to go as far as they can. They need to discuss limits on sexual behavior, praying about them and deciding on them *before* a compromising situation presents itself. In this session, you'll help your young people "draw the line" in favor of sexual behavior that pleases God.

How Far Is Too Far?

The Point

To help kids decide for themselves where God wants them to set boundaries on sexual activity and emotional commitment, in order to help them face pressures that occur when dating.

The Passages

Hebrews 13:18; II Corinthians 13:7; II Timothy 2:21, 22; Psalm 24:4, 5; 51:10; I Timothy 3:7; 5:2b; Proverbs 15:26; 16:2; 20:25; I Corinthians 7:8, 9; I John 1:9

The Preparation

You'll need the following:
• Bibles
• Pens or Pencils
• Chalk and chalkboard or newsprint and markers
• Cut-up copies of "Vital Verses" (Student Sheet 7)
• Copies of "Drawing the Line" (Student Sheet 8)

Ways of the World

Learning What "Average" Kids Say about Sex and Dating

Time for a test! It's about the way "average" teenagers in the U.S. feel about sex and dating, based on recent surveys. Note: Statistics cited are from *The Youth Ministry Resource Book* edited by Eugene C. Roehlkepartain (Group Books, 1988).

As you administer the test, write your group's answers on the board. Then write the correct answers next to your group's responses.

1. What are the top five reasons kids give for having sex before marriage? (Curiosity, 15 percent; "Everybody's doing it," 12 percent; boys pressure girls into it, 9 percent; love, 8 percent; want or need gratification, 8 percent.)

2. Before dating, some teenagers have already made up their minds that they would have sex with a date under certain conditions. What are the conditions? (If we were in love, 63 percent; if we were committed to each other, 47 percent; if we were sexually attracted to each other, 46 percent; because it's fun, 18 percent. Just 23 percent said they would never have sex with a date.)

3. What people and institutions do teenagers say have the greatest influences on their moral choices? (Self, 51 percent; family, 34 percent; school, 13 percent; church or clergy, 3 percent.)

4. What six qualities do teenagers say most attracted them to their dating partners? (Good personality, 71 percent; friendliness, 63 percent; looks, 60 percent; maturity, 45 percent; kindness, 41 percent; sense of humor, 40 percent.)

Which answers surprised you?

How do you think most Christian kids would have answered the survey questions?

When so many people seem to think it's okay to make sexual activity part of dating, it can be tough not to go along. But Jesus said that we are to be "in the world," not "of the world." That means our values and actions are to please God, even if that means being the only person who feels that way.

Let's take a "survey" of God's Word to find out what He thinks about some of these questions.

God's Guidelines

Discovering What God Has Revealed about Sexual Behavior

Pass out slips you've cut from "Vital Verses" (Student Sheet 7), at least one to each student (hand out duplicate slips if you have more kids than verses). Each student is to read his or her verse(s) and complete this sentence on the back of the slip: "This Scripture teaches that God says . . ."

After a few minutes, ask kids to read their passages and share what they have written.

Then, on chalkboard or newsprint, write: "God's Guidelines for Dating and Premarital Sex." Ask kids to help you list all the principles you and they can find in the verses.

Here are some examples; your young people may come up with others.

Hebrews 13:18—Have a clear conscience before God in all you do.

II Corinthians 13:7—Pray for strength to face temptation so that you may do what is right.

II Timothy 2:21, 22—Live a clean life so that you may be used by God for His good purposes and be prepared for good work.

Psalm 24:4, 5—We should come to worship God with a life that is pure and clean.

Psalm 51:10—God can create in us clean hearts and emotions, and give us the power to stay committed to Him and His standards.

I Timothy 3:7—A good reputation in all things, including sexual morality, keeps us from disgrace and Satan's traps.

I Timothy 5:2b—Young women (and men) need to keep themselves sexually pure, and help each other stay that way by treating each other with brotherly love.

Proverbs 15:26—Keep your thoughts pure and pleasing to God.

Proverbs 16:2—You may fool yourself into thinking that premarital sex is okay for you, but your real motives are judged by God.

I Corinthians 7:8, 9—Marriage is the right and only place for sexual intercourse.

Some people talk about "going too far" on a date. If "going all the way" (sexual intercourse) is too far, what about actions that don't go quite that far? How does a person decide how far is too far?

Let kids think about this and express opinions if they wish.

Drawing the Line
Planning Not to Be Sexually Involved in Dating

If you were driving a car and put on the brakes, how far would the car go before it reached a complete stop? (It depends on how fast you're going, how well the brakes work, and what road conditions are.)

Sexual activity is a little like that. It's a very powerful force, kind of like a really fast car. We may think we can go just short of "going too far" and hit the brakes—but the momentum keeps us going. We may feel out of control, as if we can't help going further. As a car that doesn't stop in time can cause disaster, we can end up doing something we'll always regret.

How can you plan ahead to stop a car in time? (Watch for hazards; observe the speed limit; stay far enough away from the car in front of you; don't drink or take drugs that affect your reaction time; keep the brakes fixed.)

In the same way, how can you plan ahead to stop from "going too far"? (Watch for tempting situations and avoid them; don't "speed" into a physical relationship; stay far enough away from your date and avoid too much touching; don't drink or take drugs that affect your judgment; keep reminding yourself of God's standards.)

Distribute Student Sheet 8, "Drawing the Line." Call kids' attention to Part I. Ask each person to draw "sexual limit lines" (showing "Don't touch" zones) as instructed on the sheet, and to think about whether their standards differ from God's. Avoid pressing kids to tell where they've drawn their lines.

You may want to suggest that it's a good idea to draw the line at the neck or shoulders. Touching above the neck or shoulders usually would be okay; anything below would be off limits. Some kissing and holding hands would be appropriate as the whole relationship grows. But petting (heavy or light) and erotic kissing are preparation for sexual intercourse.

What are some hazards—sexually tempting dating situations—that could be avoided? (Parking; a date at home with no one else there; excessive kissing or touching at the close of a date, etc.)

Whenever we put ourselves in a situation where all our attention is on each other's physical and sexual attraction, we open ourselves up to difficult temptation. If you find yourself in such a situation, stop and get out of it.

The best way to handle temptation is to avoid it. Decide ahead of time where you're drawing the line physically. Insist that your partner respect your limits. If he or she won't, end the date and go home.

If you feel a dating relationship is heading toward more physical intimacy, talk honestly with your partner about your values and your limits. Agree ahead of time not to tempt the other person. Increased sexual contact leads both partners to want more.

Pray with your dating partner. Honestly share your feelings. Have the courage to set limits, and ask God to help you stick to them.

For the benefit of those in your group who may already have gone "too far," you may wish to read I John 1:9. Explain that "all unrighteousness" means what it says; God has the power to forgive sexual sins as well as other sins. A fresh start is available to those who confess and turn from "going too far."

Too Far, Too Fast
Deciding Not to Get Emotionally "Hooked" Too Soon

Step 4

Sometimes we can get involved too quickly in another way—emotionally. We feel like we're "falling in love," and nothing else matters, including the mental and spiritual parts of our relationship.

Read Proverbs 20:25. **What happens if you "dedicate" or pledge your love to someone who doesn't really care about you?** (You'll probably get hurt emotionally.)

Even when both people care, a relationship can be emotionally unhealthy.

Call kids' attention to Part II of Student Sheet 8. **Let's call this the Spiral of Emotional Needs. The needs on the spiral go from the top (independent functioning) to the bottom (unable to function without the other person). At what point on this spiral does a relationship cross the line from being healthy to being unhealthy and harmful?** (Probably between "I feel special when I'm with this person" and "No one else makes me feel good like this person.")

It's great to be with a person who affirms and builds you up. But it's unhealthy to depend on a date to "make us feel good." That's surrendering our feelings to another person, and we're responsible for our own feelings. And our worth comes from God, not from the person we date.

To discover how emotionally dependent you are on a dating partner, ask yourself: Do I constantly want to know where the other person is and what he or she is doing? Do I feel anxious or upset if I see or hear about my date talking to another person of the opposite sex? Do I get upset if my date wants to go to an event without me?

If the answer is yes to most of these questions, you need to "back off" emotionally.

Discuss ways to "back off" emotionally. To the group's suggestions, you may want to add these: Talking with a counselor or other mature Christian; talking with your date about the "needs spiral" and your desire to have a healthier relationship; praying about your relationship.

Course Correction
Confessing to God

Have kids bow their heads.

If you've learned something about where you want to draw the line sexually and emotionally in dating, tell that to God.

If you feel you have gone too far sexually or emotionally in your dating relationships, tell God about it. Remember that He wants to forgive you, cleanse you, and help you obey Him (I John 1:9).

Close with a prayer for your kids—that God will help them follow through if they've decided to "draw the line" His way.

The youth meeting grinds to an emotional halt. Debbie can't stop crying. The leader finally gets her to go with him to another room. Sobbing, she tells him her story: "We broke up last night. I feel worthless. He told me that he hated me. I don't know what's wrong with me. It hurt so much! He was so cruel! And I thought he was a Christian."

Sometimes breaking up is the best thing for a dating couple to do. But is it possible to break up and remain friends? Can a Christian break up in a way that honors God and doesn't destroy the other person? How can a teenager who's been "dumped" survive emotionally?

That's what this session is about.

Breaking Up Is Hard to Do

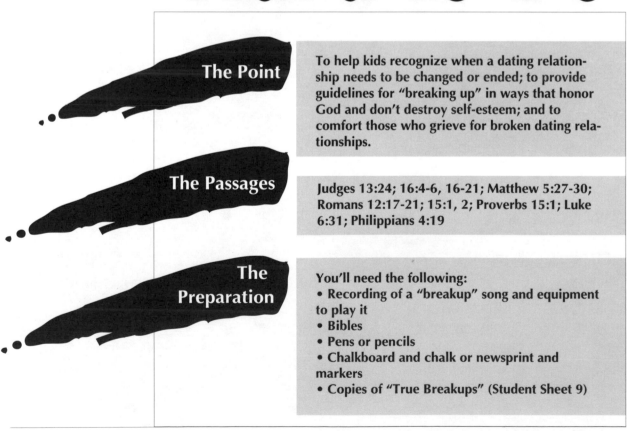

The Point — To help kids recognize when a dating relationship needs to be changed or ended; to provide guidelines for "breaking up" in ways that honor God and don't destroy self-esteem; and to comfort those who grieve for broken dating relationships.

The Passages — Judges 13:24; 16:4-6, 16-21; Matthew 5:27-30; Romans 12:17-21; 15:1, 2; Proverbs 15:1; Luke 6:31; Philippians 4:19

The Preparation — You'll need the following:
• Recording of a "breakup" song and equipment to play it
• Bibles
• Pens or pencils
• Chalkboard and chalk or newsprint and markers
• Copies of "True Breakups" (Student Sheet 9)

Splittin' Songs
Introducing the Topic of Breaking Up

Bring (or have a group member bring) and play a recording of a popular song that laments a broken romance. Or have kids come up with their own song about a breakup. Then discuss the lyrics, using questions like these:

Why did this breakup happen?

How does the singer seem to feel about the breakup? Bitter? Happy? Sad?

What does he or she want to do in response?

What are some other songs you've heard about breakups?

Why do you think there are so many of them? (Because ending a relationship is usually so painful; because so many people can identify with the subject, etc.)

As one old song says, "Breaking up is hard to do." But most people who date will experience a breakup sometime. We're going to talk about how to deal with that.

To Split or Not to Split
Discussing Why Breakups Are Sometimes Necessary

Tell the following story:

John and Karen started dating in junior high. Both went to the same church. Their parents were all friends and lived in the same neighborhood.

But John and Karen always seemed to fight when they were together. The fights got worse the longer John and Karen dated. They always seemed to be breaking up, not speaking, or making up. The rocky relationship caused their friends, who got tired of hearing about the latest conflict, to leave them alone.

It seemed that all John and Karen had left was hurt. But they kept dating and hurting each other. It was as if they dated just to cause pain, as if they enjoyed the hurt.

Do you think John and Karen should break up for good?

Allow kids to respond; avoid judging answers at this point.

Here's another story of a couple who had problems. Have kids read Judges 13:24; 16:4-6, 16-21, highlights of the story of Samson and Delilah.

Do you think Samson should have broken up with Delilah? (Yes.)

Why? (She was out to harm him; she didn't follow Samson's God; she pressured Samson to break his vow and give up his strength.)

Read Matthew 5:27-30. Explain that this passage is about separating ourselves from things or people that tempt us to sin.

How could Samson have applied this to his relationship with Delilah? (Delilah was tempting him to sin; he should have "cut her out" of his love life instead of letting her cut off his hair.)

What are some good reasons for breaking up a dating relationship today?

List responses on chalkboard or newsprint. These might include being pressured by the other person to have sex or to sin in another way; not sharing the same faith; not being able to give the other person the commitment he or she wants; seeing that the other person doesn't really care for you, etc.

Sometimes there are good reasons to break up a dating relationship. But that doesn't necessarily make it easier to do.

Splitting without Sinning
Listing Negative and Positive Ways to Break Up

What are some "classic lines" people use when they want to break off a relationship? Write kids' suggestions on the board or newsprint.
(Examples: "This really hurts me more that it will hurt you"; "Maybe we should cool the relationship awhile and try dating others just to see how much we like each other"; "Can we just be friends from now on?")

How does it feel to break up if it's your idea? (Some possibilities: awkward, painful, guilty, a relief, angry.)

What if it's not your idea? (Shocking, sad, angry, hurt, rejected, etc.)

When dating couples break up, there is often much hurt and pain. What are some ways in which people who are breaking up might purposely hurt each other?

List answers on the chalkboard or newsprint. These might include letting the person "get the message" when he or she discovers you going out with someone else; harrassing the other person with angry notes or phone calls after the breakup; saying things like, "I hate you," or "I never really liked you anyway"; criticizing the person to your friends.

While there will always be some pain, we can avoid intentionally hurting the other person. Often in trying to lessen our own hurt, we inflict pain on others. We falsely assume that by putting them down we will feel better. We may also try to be the first one to announce the breakup, putting the other person on the defensive. That way they "get hurt" first. Still, both people are often in pain.

How could you break up in a way that isn't cruel to the other person?

Have the group read each of the following Scripture passages. After each one is read, ask what guideline for breaking up could be drawn from it. List summaries like the following on the chalkboard or newsprint:

Romans 15:1, 2—Don't put down, build up.
Proverbs 15:1—Use gentle words and avoid anger.
Luke 6:31—Do to others what you'd have them do to you.

Distribute Student Sheet 9, "True Breakups." Read the case studies together and ask kids to evaluate them according to the biblical guidelines you listed. Which of the breakups could be improved by following the guidelines? How?

Summarize with comments like these: **In the negative examples (the first three), the person being rejected was hurt. The underlying assumption was, "I'll be unkind to you when I break up with you so that you'll be glad to get rid of me." When we look at our criteria of building others up, being gentle without anger, and treating others the way we'd want to be treated, we see that the last two situations tended to employ these. A letter or conversation can bring up the positive memories of a relationship and the qualities we appreciate about the other person—instead of accusing and putting the other person down.**

When You Feel Split in Two
Responding When Someone Breaks Up with Us

Look at Student Sheet 9 again. **How would you have felt if you were the "dumped" person in the first three examples?**

What options would you have in responding to being dumped? (Trying to get revenge; thinking it was your fault; becoming depressed; vowing never to care about anybody else again, etc.)

Read Romans 12:17-21. **If you were on the "receiving end" of a breakup, how could these verses guide your response?**

Allow kids to reply. As needed, supplement with information like the following:

1. *Don't try to get revenge.* It's up to God, not you, to repay evil. And hurting the other person back isn't going to mend the old relationship or get you a new one.

2. *Try to work toward a peaceful relationship.* This may mean being "just friends."

3. *Don't be too hard on yourself.* Verse 18 says, "If it is possible, as far as it depends on you . . ." A dating relationship is a two-way street; you can't maintain it without the other person's help. If the other person wouldn't cooperate in the dating relationship, its end didn't depend on you—so don't blame yourself. If you do what you can to work toward a peaceful friendship after the breakup, but the other person refuses, it's not your fault. It's good to examine your attitudes and actions to see whether you can learn something for next time, but it's destructive to blame yourself into depression.

4. *Overcome evil with good.* Instead of getting revenge, try being extra nice to the person. It will be that much harder for the person to ignore you or to see you as an enemy.

After wrapping up discussion, ask kids to bow their heads as you make comments like these: **Maybe the hardest part of breaking up is fearing that no one else will want to go out with us or care for us in the future. That can keep us from breaking off a bad relationship or keep us from recovering when we've broken up. But God knows our real needs, and promises to meet them in His own way.**

Read Philippians 4:19. Close with silent prayer, giving kids a chance to tell God about their dating mistakes of the past or hopes for the future.

Who Are You Trying to Impress?

If you agree with a statement, circle the "A" for agree.
If you disagree with a statement, circle the "D" for disagree.
If you don't know how you feel about a statement, circle the "U" for undecided.

A D U 1. My date needs to be good looking.

A D U 2. My date should be popular at school or in my group of friends.

A D U 3. It doesn't matter what my parents think about those I date.

A D U 4. My date should get along well with my group of friends.

A D U 5. My date should be impressed with having the opportunity to date me.

A D U 6. I take my dates to places that are awesome and will impress them.

A D U 7. I enjoy giving expensive gifts to my date.

A D U 8. I would never let my parents drive me around on a date.

A D U 9. I enjoy being seen in the "in" places around town with my date.

A D U 10. It isn't important whether or not my date likes to go to worship or church functions with me.

Number of times you circled "A": _____

Christian Dating?

Dating for Christians just isn't the same as for some other people. To find out some things about "Christian dating," fill in the left side of the sheet with 15 biblical attitudes from Matthew 5:1-10, Colossians 3:12-14, and James 3;17, 18. The right side of the sheet is for writing a way you could show each biblical attitude on a date.

Attitudes	Actions
1.	1.
2.	2.
3.	3.
4.	4.
5.	5.
6.	6.
7.	7.
8.	8.
9.	9.
10.	10.
11.	11.
12.	12.
13.	13.
14.	14.
15.	15.

Do You Really Go Together?

Circle YES or NO to show whether you and the people you date would agree with the following statements. If you aren't dating, answer each statement to show how you feel a dating relationship should be.

YES   NO   **1. Both believe in Jesus Christ as their personal Savior and Lord.**

Note: Stop here if you answered NO. Why? There is no spiritual-compatibility outside of Jesus Christ. Read I John 1:3. Continue if you answered YES.

YES   NO   **2. Both regularly attend church and other activities that promote spiritual growth and fellowship.**

YES   NO   **3. Both pray for and with each other.**

YES   NO   **4. Both abstain from sexual intercourse before marriage.**

YES   NO   **5. Both seek God's will for their lives and futures.**

YES   NO   **6. Both seek the guidance of the Bible, the Holy Spirit, and the Christian community when making important decisions.**

YES   NO   **7. Both sets of parents approve of this dating relationship.**

Each statement from #2 through #7 is represented as a slice in this "pie." For each **YES** answer, color in the matching slice. Leave unshaded those answered **NO.** The more shaded your circle is, the more spiritually compatible your relationship is or will be.

What Happens If . . . ?

Situation 1:

The phone rings. The person calling you for a date looks great and acts really nice. You don't know the person well. How do you find out anything about whether that person is a Christian before you accept a date? What do you say? What might you do?

Situation 2:

During lunch at school with all your friends standing around, the student body president—one of the most popular people in school—asks you to go on a date to Homecoming. You know this person is really nice, but you also know he or she has never set foot inside a church. What do you say in front of all your friends?

Situation 3:

There's a person at school—you like him or her a lot but have never dated. You would like to go out with that person on a date, but first you want to know more about that person and whether he or she is a Christian. What would be the best way to get to know that person better before you consider dating?

Situation 4:

For several months you've been dating a person from your youth group. You thought he or she was a sincere Christian. But recently you've discovered this person goes to church only because of parental pressure. You feel you are already romantically involved with the person. What do you do or say?

Your Dream Date

You've just returned from your dream date. It's been perfect! Now you're home in your room, writing about this date so that you'll never forget it. Where did you go? Who were you with?

Your Dating Circles

How do we need to grow in our dating relationships?

Socially—Enjoying going to new places and making new friends as well as being in lasting relationships with old friends.

Mentally—Sharing thoughts, values, and opinions in places that stimulate new and creative ideas.

Emotionally—Being in a setting that brings out your best and deepest feelings in an atmosphere of sharing and trust.

Spiritually—Together, getting to know God better and learning what He wants of us as individuals and couples.

Think of places you might go and things you might do on a date that fit one or more of the above definitions. Try especially to come up with settings and activities that fit both the "Spiritually" category and one or more of the others. Write these in the circles where they fit.

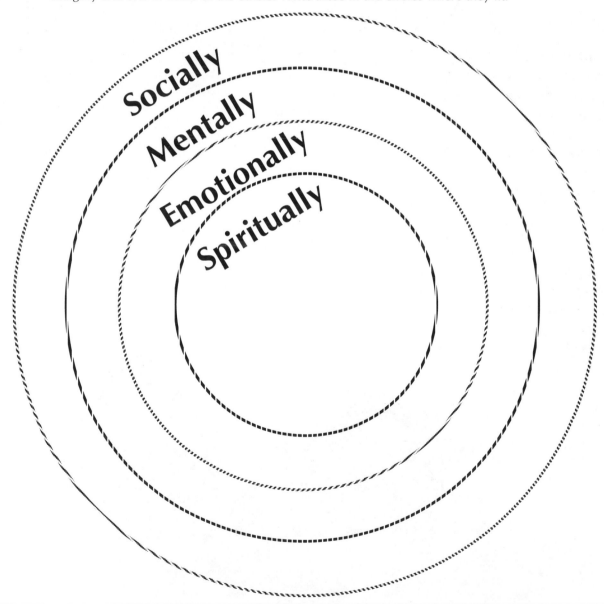

Vital Verses

Psalm 24:4,5
He who has clean hands and a pure heart, who does not lift up his soul to an idol or swear by what is false. He will receive blessing from the Lord and vindication from God his Savior.

I Corinthians 7: 8, 9
Now to the unmarried and widows I say: It is good for them to stay unmarried, as I am. But if they cannot control themselves, they should marry, for it is better to marry than to burn with passion.

II Timothy 2:21, 22
If a man cleanses himself from the latter [ignoble or sinful purposes], he will be an instrument for noble purposes, made holy, useful to the Master and prepared to do any good work. Flee the evil desires of youth, and pursue righteousness, faith, love, and peace, along with those who call on the Lord out of a pure heart.

II Corinthians 13:7
Now we pray to God that you will not do anything wrong. Not that people will see that we have stood the test but that you will do what is right even though we may seem to have failed.

I Timothy 3:7
[An overseer] must also have a good reputation with outsiders, so that he will not fall into disgrace and into the devil's trap.

Hebrews 13:18
Pray for us. We are sure that we have a clear conscience and desire to live honorably in every way.

Psalm 51:10
Create in me a pure heart, O God, and renew a steadfast spirit within me.

Proverbs 16:2
All a man's ways seem innocent to him, but motives are weighed by the Lord.

I Timothy 5:2b
[Treat] younger women as sisters, with absolute purity.

Proverbs 15:26
The Lord detests the thoughts of the wicked, but those of the pure are pleasing to him.

Drawing the Line

Part I: Physical

A. One of these figures (the guy if you're a guy, the girl if you're a girl) represents you. The other represents a person you date (or could date). Draw your "sexual limit lines" for touch and physical intimacy on your own portrait—then on your partner's portrait. Put your initials on these lines.

B. Now draw lines where you think Christ might put the limit. Put a small cross at the end of each of these lines.

C. Are your lines and Christ's the same or different? If His limit is different from yours, ask yourself why.

Part II. Emotional

Where on this spiral does a healthy dating relationship become an unhealthy one? Draw a line between two of the statements to show your answer.

I like being with this person in a group setting.

I enjoy being with this person and others on dates.

I want to date only this person.

I feel special when I'm with this person.

No one else makes me feel good like this person.

I need to be with this person in order to feel special.

True Breakups

The Rumor
One girl started a lot of untrue rumors about her boyfriend. Then she told him she could no longer date him because she had heard terrible things about him.

The Invitation
A guy wanted to break up with his girlfriend. So he asked a friend of his to invite the girlfriend to an "innocent" church event. Thinking there would be no harm to her dating relationship, the girl accepted the invitation. Then the boyfriend made a scene and broke up with her—saying it was because she'd gone out with someone else.

The Messenger
Another girl had one of her friends tell her dating partner that it was all over—instead of telling him herself.

The Rose
One guy took his date to a park and gave her a rose. He told her that she would always be special to him, but he didn't feel that dating seriously was what he needed right now. While there were tears and sadness, they prayed together and continued to be Christian friends.

The Letter
Another girl had a boyfriend, but became interested in dating someone else. She couldn't face rejecting her old boyfriend. So she wrote him a kind letter that explained her feelings. She told him how painful it would be to say this face to face, so she was writing instead. She included Scripture and prayer in her letter.

How to Talk to Kids about College Prep

by Duffy Robbins

As a youth minister-turned-college professor I can't help but notice them every fall as I walk across our campus. I can't help but remember that these new, fresh-faced freshmen wandering our campus, trying desperately to simultaneously attract attention and remain anonymous, are people who only a few weeks ago were members of somebody's youth group.

I've noticed their mixed emotions. I've heard their unspoken resolutions, their undeclared plans, and their unconfessed doubts. They and I both suspect, I think, that their adventure in these next four years will leave a life-long impression on them. Perhaps because I think like a youth minister, or because I live among them as a teacher, I've come to believe that one of our important tasks in youth ministry is to prepare our students for this new experience.

The real tests these kids face over the next few years will have little to do with Modern Civilization and Organic Chemistry. They will face tough questions for which they have been given no texts—except the preparation they received before ever setting foot on campus. That preparation is a ministry that we in youth work must not neglect.

Welcome to "What about U"

What questions and issues will your kids face if they go to college? Here's a sampling of the "curriculum" they'll have to deal with:

Identity 202. Away from old friends and family members who might never let them get away with a drastic change of lifestyle or life direction, these freshmen will be asking themselves, "Who will I be?"

Exploring one's identity begins in childhood. But during the high school and college years one must commit to an identity. There are decisions to make, vocations to choose, goals to set. The college years bring with them an ominous sense that, beginning now, the choices count. From here on out, we keep score.

Religion 101. A teenager's faith is often shaped more by the crowd around than the convictions within. The reason: Many kids have never made a personal decision to follow Christ. The youth group follows Christ, and they've followed the youth group. Or their parents follow Christ, and they've been following their parents. The college years force kids to confront the issue of whether this Christian faith is really their own—to ask, "What do I really believe?"

College students find themselves in dorms with people whose gods are very different from the god of the youth group, the god of Mom or Dad, or the God of Scripture. That's when they begin to find out whether they actually believe what they believe they believe.

Ethics 101. This "course" deals with moral choices—choices regarding sexuality, personal habits, integrity. Many high school graduates seem to have firm moral convictions, but after the first few fall weekends it's often easy to tell who has convictions and who has simply lacked sufficient opportunity for immorality.

It's one thing to decide not to have sex with your girlfriend when you don't have many opportunities to be alone anyway. But when you live in an open dorm with unlimited visiting hours, and your roommate offers to "stay lost" until tomorrow, the only thing between you and immorality is genuine moral conviction.

Too many college students have never been prepared for that kind of freedom. Their choices have been based on others' rules or a lack of opportunity. Moral values based on that kind of foundation are like the house built on sand; when temptation comes, great will be the fall.

Economics 101. College students must also begin to explore career choices and financial goals. Probably more than any other single issue, this preoccupies students the most.

College freshmen of the mid-1970s listed "the development of a meaningful philosophy of life" as a major goal for their higher education. Only one-fifth of today's freshmen have the same goal, according to a recent survey. Now the number-one target is a financially rewarding career.

Theology 100 (pre-requisite: Religion 101). This course is especially important for students who enter college with a firm commitment to the faith. Their main agenda: "Why do I believe what I believe?"

Some religion professors seem to consider fall an open season for shooting down the faith of young Christians. Sometimes the instructors intend to help students reinforce their belief in Scripture, but at other times the goal is far less positive. We need to help kids understand the reasons for belief.

If we don't, the classroom will be littered at semester's end with the scalps of frail Christians. Their faith will have been overpowered and intimidated into a back corner of their minds by some professor whose intellectual credentials proved more convincing than the lessons and flannelgraphs of Sunday School back home.

Family Life 300. Then there's the matter of meeting a mate in college. Most students would deny that they're going to college for an "MRS degree," but the fact is that many college students leave campus each spring with a diploma *and* a spouse. Long after they've agonized through the choice of a major, they'll be living with the consequences of choosing a mate.

This may not be a required course, but it's the most serious subject in the curriculum of college experience.

Building Staying Power

We often get nearsighted in youth ministry, thinking our only job is to help students survive high school. But our real goal is to equip them for the long haul—to help them develop a faith that survives and thrives apart from the umbilical cord of the youth group as they move into the college years and beyond.

As you work to prepare kids for college, consider the following suggestions:

1. Help them develop a firsthand faith. Use activities that require kids to articulate and think about their own beliefs. Some training programs only help students reflect on what their church believes; when kids move into the college years, the real issue is going to be what *they* believe.

This kind of reflection is most likely when we let kids know that the youth group is a place for *questions* of faith as well as *statements* of faith. Ask questions that force students to consider what they actually believe about the Christian faith: Why do we pray? Why is there evil in a world created by a loving and all-powerful God? Do we really have freedom to make decisions if God is all-powerful? Why is it that bad things seem to happen to good people and good things seem to work out for bad people? Don't settle for pat answers. Watch out for kids speaking "Christianese." Push them to articulate their thoughts in their own words.

Journaling is another good way to encourage this kind of growth. It forces students to reflect on

their faith, to explore their walk with Christ in their own words. A small group of students meeting weekly may provide the best context for this kind of reflection.

2. Teach them about the Christian idea of vocation—that God has called all of us to ministry. Because we have neglected this area, we are graduating students who have no idea that God is interested in their careers. They need to understand that the Wonderful Counselor wants also to be our career counselor. Some suggested passages for study: Colossians 3:23-25; I Peter 2:9, 10; Romans 12:1-12.

3. Introduce them to campus ministries. Some youth workers take each college-bound senior on a one-day field trip to the college he or she will attend. The purpose: To put the student in touch with some of the people who minister on that campus. Representatives from InterVarsity, Campus Crusade, or the Navigators would probably welcome the opportunity to have lunch with you and one of your students and share what they're doing.

4. Acquaint them with Christian literature. I doubt I would have survived the principalities and powers of my college religion courses if I hadn't been introduced to the writings of C. S. Lewis, J. I. Packer, R. C. Sproul, F. F. Bruce, John Stott, and others.

Being firmly convinced that a reading Christian is a growing Christian, I've always made it a goal to put good Christian books in the hands of my students. Most kids don't even know such books exist. It's our responsibility and opportunity to incite an interest in such reading.

5. Help them integrate their faith with real-life issues. We can't afford the luxury of acting as though our students will always face issues with easily discerned, easy-to-apply answers. We need to confront kids with slice-of-life situations that force them to think through real-life dilemmas. Case studies and role plays (like those found in resources like *Tension Getters* and *Role-a-Role* [Youth Specialties]) help students think about real-life issues they'll face at college.

6. Guide them in a study of how to discern God's will. Of special importance is helping students think through the difference between the precepts of God ("Thou shalt not commit adultery") and the principles of God ("Do not make your brother stumble"). Kids need to understand that sometimes God's guidance comes through application of the principles as much as the precepts—especially in "gray areas" and guidance dilemmas they'll face during the college years.

7. Talk honestly about the reality that many of

them will find a life partner at college. In separate small groups of guys and girls, you might want to work through a book like Walter Trobisch's *I Married You* (Harper and Row). It's an excellent primer on some of the important questions that surround this topic.

The Final Exam

Life has a way of testing our ministries—and our fruit. That is always a little discomforting, especially when those being tested are people in whom we have invested lots of love and hard work.

As you prepare your young people for college, pray through your responsibility of equipping them to meet the challenges ahead. But remember, too, that when these students leave your presence, they won't be leaving God's. "He who began a good work . . . will carry it on to completion" (Philippians 1:6).

Duffy Robbins is chairman of the department of youth ministry at Eastern College, St. Davids, Pennsylvania. A popular speaker and author, he's worked with youth groups in Rhode Island and Kentucky. His books include Hot Talks: A Youth Speaker's Sourcebook *(Youth Specialties/Zondervan).*

COLLEGE PREP

by Eric Potter

Eric Potter has plenty of college experience. While a student at Wheaton College, he served as a residence assistant. Currently a doctoral student in English at the University of Virginia, he also teaches freshman writing and American literature. Eric is also a former editor for the David C. Cook Publishing Co., where he worked on such resources as the award-winning *Senior High Pacesetter* series.

After flunking out for the third time, Allen decided college wasn't for him. Eventually he apprenticed with a plumber. Allen enjoyed that because it used his mechanical skills.

Jen went to college and loved it. She'd always wanted to be a doctor and studied hard. Her work paid off; she got into medical school.

After two weeks in college, Don figured he knew everything it had to teach him. So he quit and joined the Marines. Not until he was married and had started a family did he decide to go back to school and use his math ability by becoming an engineer.

When Debbie finished high school, she wanted to be a secretary. She started on an associate degree at a junior college, but didn't like the academic subjects. So she went to a secretarial school, which she enjoyed—and which helped her find a good job.

Someday your students may have experiences like these. Some may end up going to college; others may not.

How can you prepare kids to make decisions about going to college? This session is designed to help students examine their goals and interests and make wise choices for their futures.

To Go or Not to Go

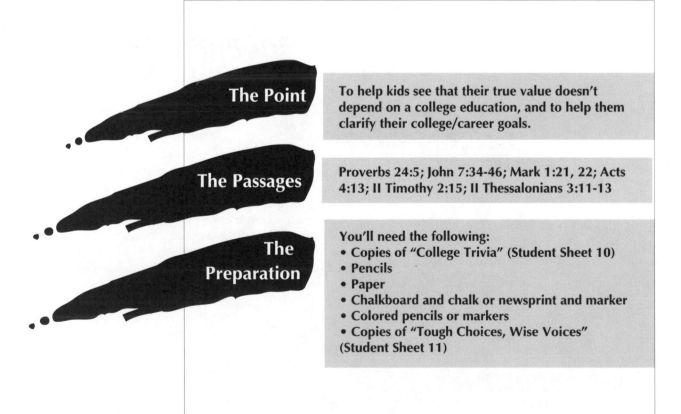

The Point

To help kids see that their true value doesn't depend on a college education, and to help them clarify their college/career goals.

The Passages

Proverbs 24:5; John 7:34-46; Mark 1:21, 22; Acts 4:13; II Timothy 2:15; II Thessalonians 3:11-13

The Preparation

You'll need the following:
• Copies of "College Trivia" (Student Sheet 10)
• Pencils
• Paper
• Chalkboard and chalk or newsprint and marker
• Colored pencils or markers
• Copies of "Tough Choices, Wise Voices" (Student Sheet 11)

Who Needs College?

Examining the Educations of Some Famous People

Give kids about five minutes to take the true/false test, "College Trivia" (Student Sheet 10). When they're finished, reveal these answers:

1. False. William Faulkner never took more than a few college classes, yet he is considered one of the greatest American writers. His work is studied throughout the world.

2. False. Einstein dropped out for awhile, but eventually earned a Ph.D. from the University of Zurich.

3. True. She also earned a doctorate in physics.

4. True. Yet she became a leader in the fight for literacy.

5. True.

6. False. Before becoming a rock star, he was a school teacher.

7. False. Iacocca earned a master's degree in mechanical engineering from Princeton.

8. True. He did, however, attend several of the most prestigious ballet schools in the Soviet Union.

9. True. He also performed many experiments on his own.

10. True.

11. False. She graduated from Sarah Lawrence College.

12. False. The opposite is true.

13. True. But his reading habit was of legendary proportions, so he was far from uneducated.

14. True.

15. False. He attended college for three years.

After going over answers, discuss:

Why did some of these people go to college while others didn't? (They had different financial resources, study habits, abilities, goals, etc.)

Are people who go to college better than those who don't? Are they more successful? Why or why not?

Help kids see that going to college doesn't determine one's value, natural ability, or potential for excellence. Students need to separate formal schooling from value as a person, from talent, and even from education.

Avoid going to the opposite extreme, however. Students shouldn't devalue college or take it lightly, since it's a necessary and valuable part of education and training for many individuals and many careers. Stress that the kind of training a person needs often depends on the kind of work he or she will do. For example, Baryshnikov may not have needed college, but he probably could not have become a great dancer without the instruction he received at various dance schools.

What do you think college is good for?

When might college be unnecessary or unhelpful?

Listen to kids' opinions without evaluating them at this point.

College Bowl

Examining the Arguments for and against College

Have students form two groups for an informal debate. One side should argue for going to college, the other against going.

Remind kids that no matter what they think about the issue, they need to present any arguments they can to help their team "win" the debate. They can use their own opinions as well as those they've heard from parents, teachers, relatives, friends, etc.

Let the debate go long enough for kids to cover a variety of arguments for and against. Have each team appoint a recorder to write down the reasons that team presents, which will help the group evaluate each argument after the debate.

In the discussion that follows the debate, help students see that there are good reasons for going and not going to college—and bad reasons, too. Here are some reasons your students are likely to come up with:

For college: It helps you get a better job; makes you a more well-rounded person; college grads make more money; college grads get more respect from people; everybody in my family went; it's fun; it's an investment in your future; it's a good place to meet someone to marry.

Against college: Nobody in my family has gone; I want to start making money right away; I don't need college for what I want to do; it's too expensive; you don't really need college to succeed.

Examine each of the arguments raised during the debate. The following questions may help.

Is this argument true?

Is this a good or bad reason for going or not going to college? Why?

What do people tend to think of those who have a college education? Of those who don't? Are these attitudes accurate? Fair?

Do you think God cares whether people go to college?

True Value
Viewing College in Light of God's Values

Asking if God cares whether someone goes to college is one way of asking what He values. The Bible doesn't say a lot about choosing careers. And it doesn't give individualized specifics like, "Be a ceramic technician," or, "Go to Princeton." But it does tell us a lot about what and who God values.

Form small groups. Assign each group one or more of the following sets of passages. Have groups read their passages and answer the following questions. You may want to write these questions on a chalkboard or newsprint for students' reference.

How would you describe the educational level of the person(s)—or types of person(s)—mentioned in this passage?

Judging from this passage, what does God value?

After groups have studied the passages and answered the questions, have each group paraphrase its passage for the rest and report its answers. When all groups have reported, continue your discussion as a larger group. The following background information may help you guide this discussion.

Group One: Proverbs 24:5, 6. This proverb appears in a section that one version calls "Sayings of the Wise." Its presence in the Bible indicates that, among other things, God values wisdom and knowledge and their importance for leaders.

Group Two: John 7:43-46 and Mark 1:21, 22. Jesus' teaching is different because He taught with authority. The teachers of the Law—the scholars or "college profs" of the day—usually spoke hesitantly, constantly citing other scholarly authorities. Jesus' authority came from God the Father, not from the kind of formal training the teachers of the Law had received. God values truth, while we tend to be impressed by diplomas.

Group Three: Acts 4:13. Peter and John were unschooled men. But the preceding verses tell us that Peter had been filled with the Holy Spirit and had spoken eloquently before the rulers, elders, and teachers of the law (sort of like addressing the President, Supreme Court, and Congress at the same time). Peter's wisdom and eloquence came from God, not from school. God values people who are willing to be used by Him no matter what their educational background.

Group Four: II Timothy 2:15; II Thessalonians 3:11-13. These verses don't say much about level of schooling, nor do they say anything about what type of work one ought to do. Instead they emphasize the kind of worker God is pleased with—one who knows how to handle the truth, works for a living, and does what is right.

After discussing the passages individually, try to draw some general conclusions about what the Bible says about value and schooling. These questions may help:

Where does our value as individuals come from? (From being made in the image of God. And, as Christians, from being bought with the blood of Christ.)

If we don't have to go to college to be of value to God, why go? (We might become more useful to Him in a particular occupation that happens to require college; it might enable us to get jobs to support ourselves; it might teach us to handle the truth, etc.)

What are some ways to gain wisdom if you don't go to college? (Reading on your own; life experience; getting to know God better; studying the Bible; learning from other people, etc.)

Know Thyself
Examining Your Own Desires

Since God tells us what kind of workers to be but not what kind of work to do, we have some freedom in choosing careers. Of course, our choice of work must fall within God's moral guidelines. For example, having a talent for blackjack doesn't mean that God wants a person to be a professional gambler.

The Bible tells us that God has given spiritual gifts to each Christian. He's also made us with personalities, talents, interests, and abilities that equip us for certain kinds of work. We need to discover these and use them.

Distribute paper and colored pencils or markers. Have each student draw a picture showing himself or herself at age 50. Encourage kids to include objects that indicate their careers—a scalpel if one wants to be a surgeon, for instance—as well as hobbies, family, etc. When kids have finished their pictures, have them ask themselves these questions:

Does college or some other kind of schooling fit in with the future I've pictured for myself? Why or why not?

If you have time, ask kids to explain their pictures to each other in small groups.

Distribute copies of "Tough Choices, Wise Voices" (Student Sheet 11) for kids to take with them and read later. Close with a prayer for God's guidance for your students, for their openness to His leading, and for hearts willing to seek His wisdom.

Choosing a college or vocational training school isn't easy. Even after a person has decided on the type of school to attend, the number of schools that seem to fit the bill is overwhelming.

Students who face this task need reassurance and sound advice. They need to know that God is concerned with their futures, including where they go to school. They also need to know that God gives them a lot of freedom in choosing a school that matches their needs.

This session can help you communicate those important messages.

Major Decisions

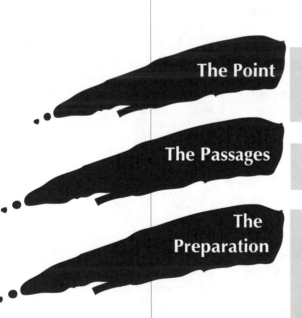

The Point

To help kids understand how to make wise college-related choices that reflect a desire to please God.

The Passages

Acts 7:22; Philippians 4:8, 9: Proverbs 1:1-7; James 1:4-8; 3:13-18; 4:2, 3

The Preparation

You'll need the following:
• **Bibles**
• **Pencils**
• **Copies of "Futures and Fries" (Student Sheet 12)**
• **Actors for the skit**
• **Chalkboard and chalk or newsprint and marker**
• **Copies of "Priorities Checklist" (Student Sheet 13)**

Tough Choices
Recognizing the Difficulty of Choosing a College and Major

Once a person has made the decision to get further education after high school, the decision-making isn't over. In fact, it's only begun. There's still the question of what kind of school or college to focus on, which particular one to pick, and which programs and majors to choose. The decisions never seem to end. Let's look in on a group of friends and see how they're coping with these major decisions.

Pass out copies of "Futures and Fries" (Student Sheet 12) to all students. Have nine volunteers (or if your group is smaller, double up on parts) perform the skit. Then discuss:

What do you think of the way these characters are choosing their schools?

What advice would you give these people?

Here are some suggestions you may want to add to the discussion.

Sally: She and her parents might compromise; she could spend her first two years at a Christian college and then transfer to one that has a veterinary program.

Ed: He was right in not worrying too much about declaring a major when he entered college, but should have spent the last year exploring options and narrowing his choices. He'd better start doing that now.

Julie: She seems to know what she's looking for, which is good. But her desire to be far from home could mean trouble if she's just looking for a chance to break all the rules she's grown up with.

John: Junior college may be a good choice for him, at least for now. Many students who need to save money, have weaker academic records, or are unsure about college start at junior colleges. Some transfer to four-year schools later.

Kay: Pursuing her interests doesn't have to mean avoiding the realities of the job market. Kay could major in art history and still take business and other "marketable" courses, too.

Jenny: Going to a small or large school is a matter of personal preference. Jenny is wise to examine the strength of the department she's interested in at her prospective colleges.

Peter: Saving money is fine, but if he expects to party all the time he won't get much of an education. He also stands a good chance of falling into a lifestyle that doesn't please God.

Alice: One could argue that some academic courses would help her grow, but not if she's uninterested in them. She could concentrate on secretarial skills now, with the possibility of other courses later.

Broaden the discussion by asking students to list other reasons or standards they've heard for choosing colleges and majors. You may want to write these on the chalkboard or newsprint. Discuss each of the reasons in terms of whether kids think it's good or bad, important or unimportant.

Biblical Wisdom
Searching for God's Priorities

Form three small groups and assign the following passages to them as noted. Encourage kids to read several verses before and after their passages to help them discover the context. They should understand their passages as thoroughly as they can before you regather the whole group.

Have each small group summarize its verses for the rest. Discuss the passages in the whole group, using questions like the following.

Group One: Acts 7:22 and Philippians 4:8, 9.

What do you think "all the wisdom of Egypt" includes? (Probably things like science, law, literature, philosophy, the arts, etc.)

How is such wisdom related to God's wisdom? (God's wisdom is always right; people's wisdom is sometimes right, and only when it doesn't contradict God's.)

How might Moses' education have prepared him for the task to which God had called him? (Helped him to be a leader, to understand people, etc.)

What kind of learning is Paul talking about in Philippians 4:9? (Christlike behavior and biblical teaching.)

What might these verses have to teach us about choosing a college and a major? (A possibility: We need to prepare for our vocations by learning from all kinds of sources, judging what we learn against the wisdom of God's Word. If we lack the ability to judge what we learn, a Christian college might help; if we lack information and experiences that some Christian schools don't provide, secular schools may help.)

Group Two: Proverbs 1:1-7 and James 3:13-18.

Where does getting wisdom or knowledge begin? (With the fear of [respect for] the Lord—recognizing His place and ours.)

How is this different from other kinds of wisdom or knowledge? (God's wisdom determines our attitudes and helps us live the way He wants us to; earthly wisdom can be stored in our heads without effect, and often leads to selfish ambition, bitterness, envy, etc.)

What do these passages indicate that God is most concerned with? (Qualities He can develop in our lives—discipline, prudence, mercy, purity, submission, etc.)

Where do things like science, philosophy, and technical knowledge fit in this picture? (Truths from these and other fields are all part of God's truth; we need godly wisdom to use these kinds of knowlege correctly.)

Group Three: James 1:4-8 and James 4:2, 3.

What does wisdom mean in this passage? (Insight that helps us face trials with joy.)

How does one get wisdom? (By asking God for it.)

What, according to these passages, is God concerned with? (Helping us to become mature and complete; the strength of our faith and purity of our motives; the way we use what we've been given.)

What could these verses have to do with choosing colleges? (Keep God's goals in mind; ask yourself whether a particular college is likely to encourage your spiritual growth or stunt it; plan to use what you learn for God's glory, not just your own comfort.)

Are you frustrated because the Bible says a lot about wisdom but very little about choosing a college or a major? These passages show that God is mainly concerned with how we live and the kind of people we become. He wants our values and priorities to be in line with His. He gives us a lot of freedom with the specifics.

That doesn't mean God finds schooling unimportant. After all, He used the training Moses probably received in governing to equip him for leading the Israelites. God also used the apostle Paul's education; Paul quoted at least four secular poets in his preaching and writing (Acts 17:28; I Corinthians 15:33; Titus 1:12).

Choosing a College
Sharing Practical Advice about Choosing Colleges

When it comes to choosing colleges and majors, God wants us to match our priorities to His. How can we do that? (We need to know the general priorities He's mentioned in the Bible; we need to pray for wisdom and to know what direction to take.)

Then we can use the minds He's given us to evaluate our options.

Ask kids to list the steps one should go through in evaluating and choosing schools. Write their suggestions on the chalkboard or newsprint. You may be amazed at how much they already know. If possible, appoint a secretary and get his or her notes typed to distribute later for kids' reference.

The following questions may help stimulate kids' list-making.

What kinds of schools can you choose from? (Technical, vocational, trade school, liberal arts college, two-year or four-year, Christian or not, Bible college, large or small, public or private, etc.)

How can you find out about the type of school you want to attend? (Get list of schools, school handbooks, and catalogs; write admissions office; use services that match you with schools; contact alumni associations to get in touch with current and former students; visit campus.)

What standards can you use in narrowing the choice? (Academics; facilities; social life; sports; distance from home; costs; community; size; campus atmosphere; extracurricular activities, etc.)

What to do in applying? (Take tests such as the S.A.T. and/or A.C.T.; decide how many schools to apply to, usually six to eight; apply to your first choice first; pick a "safety" school—one you'd be willing to attend and are positive you can get into; set up a timetable to make sure you meet deadlines.)

Choosing a Major (optional)
Reassuring Those Who Haven't Chosen Yet

Though students don't need to choose a major to get accepted into a school, some may express interest in this topic. If so, you might want to explain several things about choosing a major:

1. Colleges don't turn you down just because you don't know your intended major when you apply.

2. Most schools don't require students to officially declare a major until the end of their sophomore year. Some schools use an intended major to match students with an academic adviser, however.

3. Most students change majors at least once—some two or three times.

4. Most majors, especially in the humanities and many sciences, don't translate into training for a specific job. They don't need to.

5. Majors are a lot more flexible than many people think. For example, you can major in English and still get into medical school as long as you take the necessary science requirements.

Encourage students to major in a subject they enjoy studying. In the long run, they'll get more out of college. You may also want to remind kids that it's possible to change careers later in life; people aren't necessarily locked into the fields in which they majored in college.

Step 5

Setting Priorities
Discovering and Examining Your Priorities

To help students begin thinking about the kind of school they want to attend, distribute "Priorities Checklist" (Student Sheet 13) and have them fill it out. Then have them evaluate their priorities by answering, to themselves, the following question:

How do these priorities fit with the things that are important to God?

As needed, remind kids of God's priorities as found in the verses you studied. To close, point out the resource list at the bottom of the student sheet, which could help kids as they begin looking for and evaluating colleges.

College life is a great unknown, one that can be exciting—and terrifying. For some Christian students the prospect of attending a state university—that alleged den of secular philosophy, drug and alcohol abuse, and sexual immorality—can be especially frightening.

Students can also err in the opposite direction, painting too rosy a picture of college life in general and Christian colleges in particular. For example, some may mistakenly expect a Christian college to resemble a Christian camp or perpetual youth group meeting where people sit around playing guitars and singing Gospel songs.

While many college-related fears and expectations may be grounded in reality, they do not represent the experiences your college-bound students will have most of the time. These misconceptions often lead kids to worry about the wrong things—and distract them from preparing for the challenges that actually face them. This session can help bring the "alien" aspects of college life into sharper focus for your group members.

Life on Planet X

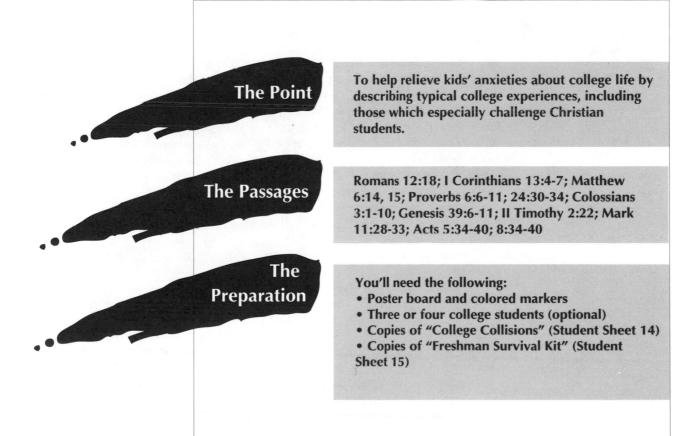

The Point

To help relieve kids' anxieties about college life by describing typical college experiences, including those which especially challenge Christian students.

The Passages

Romans 12:18; I Corinthians 13:4-7; Matthew 6:14, 15; Proverbs 6:6-11; 24:30-34; Colossians 3:1-10; Genesis 39:6-11; II Timothy 2:22; Mark 11:28-33; Acts 5:34-40; 8:34-40

The Preparation

You'll need the following:
• Poster board and colored markers
• Three or four college students (optional)
• Copies of "College Collisions" (Student Sheet 14)
• Copies of "Freshman Survival Kit" (Student Sheet 15)

Where No Kid Has Gone Before
Discussing Students' Views of College Life

Form groups of three or four. Give each group poster board and colored markers.

Each group is to draw a poster that depicts what its members think college life is like. Kids can include as many people, buildings, and activities as they have time and talent for. Provide a few suggestions to get them started if needed (for example, they might want to draw a dorm or fraternity house), but don't give them too much help. You want their perceptions, no matter how uninformed they might be.

Encourage kids to be honest about what they think goes on at college—not just drawing what they think parents and youth group leaders or Sunday School teachers want to talk about. But caution them to use care in depicting questionable activities.

When students are finished with their posters, or it's time to move on to the next step, have kids explain what they've drawn. Use the following questions to help you discuss:

What do the posters have in common?
How are they different?
What things in the posters make you want to go to college?
What things make you worried about going to college?

Landing Party
Discovering What College Is Really Like

For this step, choose one of the following options.
Option One
Having discussed some of our expectations and perceptions of what college is like, let's turn to a panel of experts to get the real story.

If possible, give kids a few minutes to come up with a list of questions—or at least to talk about the kinds of things they want to find out about college life. Encourage kids to be honest in their questions.

Bring your panel (three or four college students you've contacted before the session) to the front. In choosing your panel, try for a variety of experience (junior college, Christian college, large state university, technical school, etc.), so that your students will see the variety and similarity of college experience. If current college students are unavailable, try to find recent graduates whose memories of college are still fresh and whose experiences will seem relevant to your group members.

If kids have trouble coming up with questions, you might use some of the following.

What is your typical day like?
How much time do you spend studying? Is it enough?
What was the hardest thing about your first semester?
What are the biggest differences between high school and college?
If you could redo anything that you've done since being in college, what would it be?
What has been your biggest academic challenge?
Your biggest non-academic challenge?

Encourage panel members to be honest in their answers, but give them the option of declining to answer any questions they find too personal or which otherwise make them feel uncomfortable.

Option Two

Continue the discussion of the Step One posters by sharing your own experiences at college or those of others you know. Help students get a better picture of what college is like, how it differs from high school, and what challenges it will offer.

As needed, regardless of which option you used, summarize the following information for your students. Observe that many of the challenges that college students face fall into one of these categories:

1. *Roommates/Relationships.* One of the biggest differences between college and high school, and one of the biggest challenges and sources of conflict is having a roommate. Suddenly a student is forced to live with a total stranger who often differs from him or her in every way possible—race, geographical origin, subculture, interests, personal habits, values, tastes in music, etc. Students need to recognize this aspect of college life and prepare to meet the challenge.

2. *Responsibility/Time-Management.* Another difference between high school and college is the amount of time spent in class. College students spend, at most, a third of the time in the classroom that high school students do. All this "free time" seems wonderful to incoming freshman until they realize, often too late, that it was time they should have used for studying. The actual college work load is often twice that of the high school load.

Freedom can cause other problems. College students have no one to get them up, tell them when to go to bed, or remind them to study. College professors, unlike high school teachers, seldom remind students to keep up with their work. Many students who lack self-discipline quickly wear themselves out physically and fall behind academically.

3. *Lifestyle.* Another freedom facing college students is that of choosing their own lifestyles. Without parents or other relatives to answer to, college students can seem to get away with most anything they please. The opportunity for sin, especially when it's encouraged by peers, presents a strong challenge for students.

4. *Faith/Beliefs.* Many students find their faith and beliefs challenged in high school, but the challenge is often stronger in college. A new environment tends to make students more uncertain about everything. Roommates, dorm mates, professors, and textbooks which are indifferent or hostile to Christianity, or which question its validity, prove a strong challenge to many students—especially those not firmly grounded in their understanding of the Bible.

Step 3

Prime Directives
Exploring God's Principles for College (and Other) Living

Each of the following sets of passages is related to one of the four challenges noted in Step Two. Have a volunteer read each passage; discuss what the verses say about the way God wants us to live—and the advice they give to help us live accordingly.

Set One: Romans 12:18; I Corinthians 13:4-7; Matthew 6:14, 15.

What do these verses say about how God wants us to live?

Which of these qualities could help you get along with a roommate?

(These verses emphasize being at peace with and loving others. They also instruct us to be forgiving. College students need to practice all of these things, along with compromise and flexibility, in order to get along with roommates.)

Set Two: Proverbs 6:6-11; 24:30-34.

What is a "sluggard"? (A lazy person, one who fails to prepare for the future.)

How could a college student be a sluggard? (By sleeping instead of going to class or studying; failing to prepare for tests, etc.)

What does this verse say about how we should live in college?
(Students should use time wisely—not just to get good grades, but because diligence in all of life's tasks honors God.)

Set Three: Colossians 3:1-10; Genesis 39:6-11; II Timothy 2:22.

What specific activities do these verses condemn? Encourage students to express these activities in contemporary terms.

Which of these might you find at college? (Probably all of them.)

How might Joseph avoid sin if he were a college student today? (Probably by avoiding tempting situations and even running from them. But that doesn't mean he'd avoid college or stay in his dorm room; he learned how to survive in a very "secular" setting.)

Set Four: Mark 11:28-33; Acts 5:34-40; 8:34-40.

What kinds of responses did people give to Christ and the Gospel in these passages? (Non-committal, indifferent, hostile, and accepting.)

What other responses to the Gospel does the Bible tell us about? (Some examples: Stephen was stoned to death for his preaching. Peter and John were flogged, yet praised God for having been counted worthy to suffer.)

Which of these responses would you expect to get from people at college? (They may not hurt you physically, but they might ridicule your beliefs. Others may be indifferent or even accepting. Whatever the response, we're called to be honest about our faith.)

Flight Simulator
Practicing Responses to College Problems

To help kids practice applying the biblical principles they've studied, have them do the role plays found on "College Collisions" (Student Sheet 14). Distribute this sheet and try to involve each student in at least one role play.

Then discuss the "solutions" presented by the participants.

How effective was each solution?

How did it reflect the Scriptures we looked at earlier?

What are some other ways a person could handle such a problem?

After wrapping up discussion, distribute copies of "Freshman Survival Kit" (Student Sheet 15). This sheet lists helpful hints for first-time college students.

Close in silent prayer, encouraging kids to tell God about their college fears and hopes.

College should be a time of challenge, stretching, and growth for students. And no matter where they go to school, today's students face challenges.

They face moral challenges—pressures to abuse alcohol and drugs, to engage in premarital sex, and to live lives of self-absorption. They also face intellectual challenges to their faith.

True growth seldom occurs without challenge. But challenge should stretch, not destroy, a student's faith and obedience. Students need personally to believe the Gospel and commit themselves to Christ's lordship over their thoughts and actions. Only such a commitment will enable them to steer the narrow path between complacency and surrender.

This session is designed to help students begin to prepare for intellectual challenges to their faith—so that they can stretch without snapping.

Surviving In a Stretching World

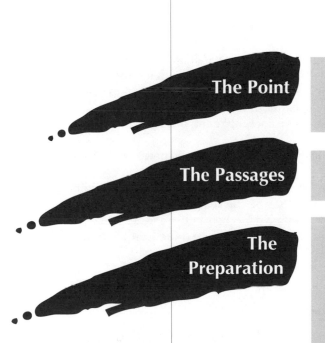

The Point

To motivate kids to prepare for campus challenges to their beliefs, and to help them see the importance of "owning their own faith" in that process.

The Passages

Acts 17:16-23, 32-34; Mark 12:13-34; II Corinthians 13:5; Psalm 16

The Preparation

You'll need the following:
- Materials for Step 1 (optional)
- Paper and colored markers
- Bibles
- Copies of "Test the Spirits" (Student Sheet 16)
- Copies of "Look Out For . . ." (Student Sheet 17)
- Modeling clay or aluminum foil

A Stretching Experience (optional)
Seeing the Tension and Value of Stretching

Start the session with one of the following: (1) a taffy pull; (2) stretching exercises; or (3) a contest to see who can be the first to blow a balloon up so large that it pops. Then discuss the role that stretching played in the activity.

How is stretching useful? (It can make things and people stronger, more flexible, or more useful.)

When is it painful? (When you're not used to it or you're not ready for it.)

What are some ways that you've been "stretched" in your life? (Did something scary to learn a new skill, learned to get along with an irritating person, etc.)

Stretching can be scary—but good for us. We're going to talk about how college can force us to stretch—and grow.

Stretch-a-Sketch
Discovering Challenges Students Expect to Face

College is a stretching time; it's supposed to be. This is especially true for Christians who, on top of all the usual challenges, face challenges to their faith. Let's start today by finding out what kinds of college challenges you expect, and maybe fear, to face.

Form groups of four. Distribute paper and colored markers. Instruct each group to come up with a list of at least five challenges to faith that a Christian student probably will face at college. (Some possibilities: invitations to use drugs, get drunk, have sex, watch pornography; work load that crowds out prayer and Bible reading; temptation to skip church; professors who mock Christianity; people who say it doesn't matter what you believe; people who view Christianity as part of our culture but not as the truth; people who deny God's existence, etc.)

When groups have finished their lists, have them pick one of their toughest challenges and draw a cartoon or comic strip that illustrates the challenge and a possible way to handle it. Then have each group display and explain its drawing. Discuss the cartoons and the groups' lists.

How are these challenges like and unlike the ones you already face at school?

How might being at college make it harder to handle these challenges? (Further from home, church, etc.)

How might the challenges at a Christian college be different from those at a state university? How might they be the same? (At a Christian college, you might be tempted to drift along with what others believe instead of examining your own faith; at a secular school, you might face more hostility to Christian beliefs.)

Scripture Stretch
Examining How Jesus and the Apostles Handled Challenges

At one time or another we'll all face challenges to the Gospel and to our faith. We shouldn't be surprised when this happens. After all, the apostles and even Jesus Himself faced such challenges. Knowing that they did can give us

encouragement; learning how they handled these challenges can prepare us for the future.

Have a volunteer read each of the following passages. In discussing the passage, encourage students to discover the nature of the challenge and the method the apostles or Christ used to meet it. Kids should then relate it to a contemporary situation, preferably one of the cartoons drawn earlier.

Acts 17:16-23, 32-34:

How would you compare this situation to college? (People were "into" discussing philosophy and other ideas.)

Why do you think Paul chose to talk about the "unknown" god? (It was a chance to talk about the true God.)

What were the different responses to his message? (Rejection, ridicule, curiosity, openness, belief.)

Mark 12:13-34:

What three types of challengers or questioners did Jesus face? (Possible answer: Those who wanted to trap Him, those who disagreed with Him, and those who really wanted His answer.)

Which do you think you'd find in college today? (Probably all of them.)

How did Jesus respond to them? (With cleverness, wisdom, and knowledge of God and Scripture.)

How might you prepare to follow His example? (Study to have a better knowledge of the Bible; work on a closer relationship with God; practice responses you might make, etc.)

Stretching Situations
Practicing Responses to Likely Challenges

Distribute copies of "Test the Spirits" (Student Sheet 16). Have volunteers read the sheet aloud. Discuss questions if they arise.

Then pass out copies of "Look Out For . . ." (Student Sheet 17). As a group, discuss each character on the sheet, concentrating on how kids might respond if confronted by that character. Urge students to use what they learned from the Bible passages and Student Sheet 16 in responding to the people and challenges represented. Point out that some of the characters believe things that many Christians would agree with, at least in part; discuss separating the good and bad.

As needed, add information like this to the discussion:

Owen Open-Minded. Owen is hardly open-minded. Everyone has a world view, and every world view excludes at least some other views. In Owen's case, he excludes the views of parents and anyone else who disagrees with him. What's important is to bring our views into line with the reality that's revealed in the Bible.

Gary Granola. In Gary's case we need to separate the wheat and the chaff. Concern for the environment and treatment of animals can be ways of being stewards of God's earth, and God commands us to live at peace with others. But brotherhood with animals tends toward pantheism (the belief that God is only a force which is present in everything). And there can be no real peace apart from Christ.

Mary Missionary. Mary's desire to serve God is praiseworthy, but her attitude toward other fields of study falsely separates work into "spiritual" and "secular." She also needs to see the value of preparing so that God can use her to her fullest potential.

Quentin Questioner. Questions can be honest, but Quentin seems to question the Bible not to discover truth but to defend the lifestyle he's living or wants to live.

Ingrid Intellectual. This view of Christianity is common in many academic circles. It assumes that Christianity cannot be different from other faiths. It fails to recognize Christianity's claim to be the truth about reality.

Patrick Progressive. Ignoring God and His truth, Patrick is left with the uneasy freedom of being his own boss. With God out of the picture, people become their own little gods. And imperfect, limited people make pretty awful Supreme Beings.

Ursula Utopia. Again we must separate wheat and chaff. Ursula's concerns about helping the poor and loving others echo biblical concerns. But her utopian vision of society conflicts with the Bible, which says people are born in sin, that salvation comes from Christ, and that heaven will be in heaven.

Charlie Churchcrusher. Sadly, many of his criticisms of the church are true. As Christians we need to acknowledge our shortcomings and seek to live as God wants us to. We must also help people like Charlie see that God doesn't approve of everything that's been done in His name.

Stretching Yourself
Examining Our Own Faith

When some kids go to college, they discover that the faith that seemed so real in high school was really only a church-going habit they'd picked up from their parents. If you're not really a Christian or if your faith isn't very strong, you won't be prepared to meet college challenges to your faith.

Read II Corinthians 13:5, in which Paul instructs us to examine ourselves. Discuss with kids how we can do that. Then help them to begin examining their own lives with one of the following options.

Option One: Give each student a lump of clay or a piece of aluminum foil. Each student should make a sculpture that represents his or her relationship with God. For example, a weak relationship might be symbolized by a tottering tower; a growing relationship might be represented by a leaf. Encourage kids to pray silently about this relationship.

If you have time and your students feel comfortable sharing, have them show and explain their sculptures in groups of two or three. Encourage them to pray for each other.

Option Two: Give your students time to silently think and pray about their relationship with God.

Final Stretch
Remembering God's Help in Stretching Times

Have students look up Psalm 16. Ask a volunteer to read it. Discuss briefly how this Psalm can serve as an example of a proper reliance on God and as a comfort in knowing God's faithful care for His children. Remind kids that David faced many challenges in his life: He fought Goliath, suffered political oppression, ruled a nation, fought battles, committed adultery, suffered God's wrath, raised a son who murdered his brother, and was briefly overthrown by his own son. But David knew that he could trust God for support and protection.

Close in prayer; ask God to help kids in the stretching days ahead.

College is a time of increased independence. Students who live at college are especially uprooted from home environments and their built-in support systems of parents, family, and home church. This uprooting is, in a way, a necessary part of growing up.

Yet uprooting can also cause problems. It may reveal that what appeared to be genuine Christian faith was merely family habit—that the student had not "owned" his or her faith.

Even when a student's faith is very real, it needs support and nurture. Recognizing our need for fellowship, encouragement, and accountability, God commands us to keep meeting together. Students need a new system of Christian support when they're away at college. This session encourages them to develop one.

On Your Own

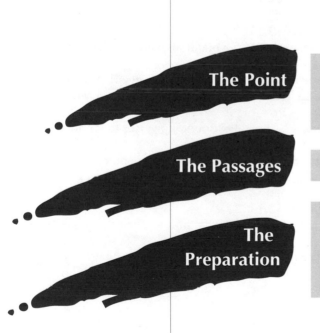

The Point	To help kids see the value of trusting God and maintaining fellowship with other Christians when they go off to college, and to encourage them to make specific plans to do so.
The Passages	Acts 2:42; Hebrews 10:23-25; Daniel 6:16-23
The Preparation	You'll need the following: • Bibles • Copies of "What If?" (Student Sheet 18) • Chalkboard and chalk or newsprint and marker

Step 1

Everybody Needs Somebody

Experiencing Our Dependence on Others

Have students form a circle and hold hands. Next, have each person let go of one hand he or she is holding, reach into the center of the circle, and take hold of someone else's hand. Then tell kids to get back into a circle—without releasing the hands they're holding.

Kids will soon discover they're in a knot. It will be difficult to get back into a circle, but not impossible.

Let the group struggle until kids figure out the solution for themselves (most eventually do). If they're still in a knot after a sufficient amount of struggling, advise them to stop struggling individually, choose one person to get untangled, and then one by one follow that person's lead. Eventually kids should untie the knot.

When the group is untangled, have kids take their seats and discuss:

Why was it difficult to get undone?

What complicated the procedure?

How did you finally get free?

In a knot like this, people usually struggle individually at first to free themselves. When this doesn't work, they discover that they have to work together and help each person get free.

It's important to get help from others when you want to get out of a knot. It doesn't work to "go it alone." That's true with college life, too. Let's see what the Bible says about having a support system of other Christians.

Step 2

Focus on Fellowship

Exploring God's View of Fellowship

Have someone read Hebrews 10:25.

→ **Why, according to this verse, should we maintain Christian fellowship?** (To encourage each other.)

What kind of encouragement might a college student need? (Help with homesickness; encouragement to live for Christ despite pressure; answers for tough questions, etc.)

Have someone read Acts 2:42. Look at surrounding verses to see that this passage describes early believers.

→ **According to this passage, what are some benefits of spending time together as Christians?** (Receiving instruction; having fellowship; eating together; taking Communion; praying.)

Have someone read Hebrews 10:23, 24.

→ **What does this passage tell us to do?** (Stay faithful to Christ; spur each other to love and good deeds.)

→ **How can meeting together as Christians help us do these things?** (We can cheer each other up when we're discouraged or tired; check up on how we're doing; be accountable to each other; remind each other of what's important; arrange to do good deeds together, etc.)

Have someone read Daniel 6:16-23.

How could going to college feel like being thrown into a lions' den? (You could feel threatened by the work load, the unfamiliar setting, people who are hostile to your faith, etc.)

→ **If you were in a lions' den, would you rather be alone or with other people who cared about you? Why?** (Other people could help protect and encourage you, etc.)

God could have shut the lions' mouths without sending an angel. Why do you think He sent the angel? (Maybe as a visible encouragement to Daniel, even to keep him company.) Observe that we, too, need the visible encouragement of people who are "on our side."

How Sweet It Is
Discussing the Benefits of Christian Fellowship

Some of us have a pretty good support group built up—parents, siblings, youth leaders, church friends, etc. There's usually somebody around to help us when we have problems. But when we go to college, especially if it's away from home, things are different. All of a sudden we're uprooted. If we don't take action to "re-root" ourselves in our new college environment, we could, like a plant, just shrivel up spiritually.

To help kids see the difference having Christian fellowship and support can make when facing college problems, distribute copies of "What If?" (Student Sheet 18). Read each situation and discuss it as a group.

In all these cases, Christians can pray for their friends in need. Prayer is one of the most powerful ways to love each other. We can encourage each other, talk things through, help each other find answers, remind each other of what we've learned from God's Word, and laugh and cry together.

Planning to Get Together
Discovering Christian Fellowship Opportunities

To benefit from fellowship, we have to have it in the first place. We need to discover ways to re-root ourselves at college.

Using a chalkboard or newsprint to record ideas, have students brainstorm all the possibilities for college fellowship they can think of. You may want to keep this list, type it, and distribute copies at a later date.

Some opportunities to include:

• A local church and its college group. Many churches also have an "adopt-a-student" program that offers a "substitute" Christian family.

• A denominational student group.

• Parachurch organizations like InterVarsity Christian Fellowship, Campus Crusade for Christ, Fellowship of Christian Athletes, and the Navigators.

• Reading and writing to magazines like *Campus Life*.

• A dorm Bible study.

• A Christian fraternity or sorority (there are a few).

If time allows, share some of the following ideas that your group could be involved in *before* college. If possible, choose one or more to do in the near future.

1. After getting a college-bound student's approval, write to the pastor of the church your student plans to attend. Introduce your student and encourage the pastor to welcome the student and help him or her get involved.

2. Your group could start an adopt-a-student program. Individuals or small groups would commit themselves to writing (or sending tapes) to a student who's away at college (or joined the military or moved away to work). These letters or tapes could provide news from home, an update on the youth

group's activities, and encouragement such as Bible verses, songs, summaries of sermons, poems, etc.

3. College-bound members of your group could plan a round-robin letter in which they compare notes on their college experiences, share advice, give and receive encouragement, and remind each other of the importance of serving God.

Close in prayer, praying for your college-bound students by name.

College Trivia

Read each statement below and show whether you think it's true or false by circling the appropriate word on the left

TRUE   FALSE   1. Novelist William Faulkner graduated from the University of Mississippi with a degree in philosophy.

TRUE   FALSE   2. Albert Einstein flunked out of college.

TRUE   FALSE   3. Former astronaut Sally Ride earned a bachelor's degree in English.

TRUE   FALSE   4. Barbara (Mrs. George) Bush attended Smith College but did not graduate.

TRUE   FALSE   5. Martin Luther King, Jr's. highest degree was a Ph.D. in systematic theology from Boston University.

TRUE   FALSE   6. Rock singer Sting dropped out of high school after forming his first band.

TRUE   FALSE   7. Lee Iacocca went to college for only one year.

TRUE   FALSE   8. Russian-born dancer Mikhail Baryshnikov never went to college.

TRUE   FALSE   9. Thomas Alva Edison, inventor, received only three months of formal education and four years of teaching by his mother.

TRUE   FALSE   10. Filmmaker Spike Lee graduated from Morehouse College before attending New York University's film school.

TRUE   FALSE   11. Instead of graduating from college, TV interviewer Barbara Walters started as a newsroom secretary and worked her way up from copy editor to reporter to anchorperson.

TRUE   FALSE   12. The average full professor (highest position) makes approximately twice the yearly salary of the average airline pilot.

TRUE   FALSE   13. Abraham Lincoln's formal schooling did not amount to more than one year.

TRUE   FALSE   14. Alice Walker, author of *The Color Purple,* earned a bachelor's degree from Sarah Lawrence College.

TRUE   FALSE   15. Basketball star Michael Jordan was drafted by the Chicago Bulls right out of high school.

Choosing a Career

You don't have to pick your career right this minute—but it's good to start thinking in advance about occupations that might fit you. Here are some suggestions for making career choices.

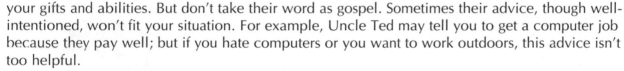

1. *Pray.* Ask for God's wisdom in discovering your abilities and exploring career options. Tell Him you want to serve Him in whatever way He wants. (If you don't want that, are you really looking for His guidance?)

2. *Examine yourself.* What are your likes, dislikes, interests, and abilities? What have been your most rewarding experiences? Since we usually like what we're good at, interests and accomplishments are good indicators of our abilities and can point us toward rewarding careers.

3. *Talk to parents and relatives.* Ask them what they think you might be good at. These people know you well. They have watched you over the years and probably have a lot of insight into your gifts and abilities. But don't take their word as gospel. Sometimes their advice, though well-intentioned, won't fit your situation. For example, Uncle Ted may tell you to get a computer job because they pay well; but if you hate computers or you want to work outdoors, this advice isn't too helpful.

4. *Consult your guidance counselor.* School counselors often have information about various career options, the kind of training involved, and which colleges and vocational schools provide that training. Your counselor may also have tests and computer programs that help you discover aptitudes and match them with careers.

5. *Go to the library.* Most libraries (try the reference section) have books on careers in general and on specific occupations. If there's a college or university nearby, find out whether it has a career planning office that makes resources available to non-students.

7. *Try Intercristo* (or some other placement organization). Intercristo is a Christian career network. It gives applicants an aptitude test and, based on the results, matches applicants with currently available jobs. Address: 19303 Fremont Avenue North, Seattle, WA 98133-0016.

8. *Volunteer for an internship.* If you are interested in being a doctor or nurse, for example, try volunteering as an aide at a local hospital. Your reaction to being around hospitals and sick people may tell you something about whether you should try medical or nursing school.

Some Helpful Books

What Color Is Your Parachute? by Richard Nelson Bolles (Ten Speed Press). The author writes that since we usually like what we're good at, examining the experiences we've enjoyed is a key to discovering our interests. He provides many helpful exercises to aid in this discovery process. He also gives good advice about the job market and matching one's interests to a career—or creating a job to fit one's abilities. The book is frequently revised and updated, so the most recent edition will be most helpful.

The Almanac of Jobs and Salaries. Covers a broad range of jobs, which is a good way to learn what's out there. Provides brief descriptions and wage information.

Dictionary of Occupational Titles. U.S. Dept. of Labor. Revised frequently. Gives job titles and descriptions.

Occupational Outlook Handbook. U.S. Dept. of Labor. Revised yearly. Provides information on training, working conditions, nature of work, qualifications, etc.

Encyclopedia of Careers and Vocational Guidance. William E. Hopke, editor-in-chief.

Futures and Fries

The Cast:

BOB   JOHN
SALLY   KAY
ED   JENNY
JULIE   PETER
           ALICE

The Setting:

Fast food restaurant, Christmas break. A group of students is seated around a table with Bob, the youth leader.

BOB: Has anybody seen my fries? *(No answer. He talks to himself.)* I'm sure I ordered a large fries. They've got to be here somewhere. *(He addresses the group again.)* So, what are all of you going to do with the rest of Christmas break?

SALLY: I'm going to fill out college applications.

ED: Where are you applying?

SALLY: I'm not sure yet. My parents want me to go to a Christian college, but I want to be a vet. The state university's got a great pre-vet program, but my parents really want me to go to a Christian school.

JULIE: Well, I don't care if my college is Christian or not as long as it's far away from home, and has a marching band and a good business program.

JOHN: You're not asking for much, huh?

JULIE: Well, I could go to Out-of-State University. That's where my boyfriend goes. But I don't know.

BOB: I met my wife in college. *(He sighs.)* Did anybody find an extra order of fries? *(No one answers.)*

JOHN *(ignoring Bob)* : I wish I could go to Upscale College. That's where all my friends are going, but I don't have the money. I'll probably go to the junior college for two years and then transfer. I guess that's okay. Besides, I don't know what I want to major in.

ED: Hey, picking a college is the easy part. I went to Big State because all my friends are there. And you don't have to have a major right away. You don't have to pick one until spring semester of your sophomore year.

KAY: You're a sophomore now, just like me. So what major are you going to declare?

ED: I don't know. I thought maybe pre-law, and then I thought pre-med, and then anthropology, or maybe education . . .

KAY: Well, I want to major in art history. But my parents say it isn't marketable. I know they're right, in a way, but it's really what I want the most.

JENNY: I want to study psychology. So I'm checking out departments at different schools. There are so many to choose from. The only thing I know for sure is that I want to go to a small college.

BOB: I went to a small college. I really loved it. *(He looks around.)* I know I ordered large fries.

PETER: Well, size isn't important to me. I want to go to Moosehead U.

ALICE: That's such a party school!

PETER: That's why I picked it! Besides, it's cheap.

ALICE: Oh, great reasons! Though I shouldn't talk. I don't even want to go to college. I just want to be a secretary.

JOHN: You could come to the junior college with me.

ALICE: No thanks. I don't want to take academic subjects. I just want to learn secretarial skills.

BOB *(desperately)*: Has anybody seen my fries?

ALL *(irritated, looking at BOB)*: No!!!

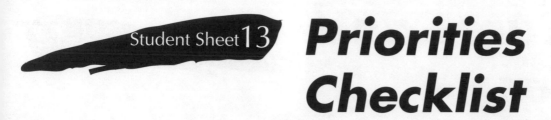

Priorities Checklist

Answer the following questions about the kind of school you'd like to attend. Then number the questions in the order of their importance to you in choosing a college (with number one being most important, etc.).

**Importance
to you**

_____ What kind of school (community college, vocational/technical school, state university, private college, Ivy League university, other) do you think you and your parents can afford? Be sure to take financial aid into consideration.

_____ How far from home would you like your school to be?

_____ Do you want to go to a Christian college?

_____ What size school would you like to attend?

_____ What kind of academic reputation do you want for your school?

_____ Describe the kind of campus atmosphere (friendly, challenging, politically active, spiritually sensitive, etc.) you'd like.

_____ What kind of social life do you prefer?

_____ What kind of sports program do you want your school to have?

_____ What geographical location do you prefer (city, country, mountains, seaside, etc.)?

_____ What kind of facilities (computers, theater, library, labs, etc.) do you require?

_____ If you know your intended field of study, how strong would you like your school to be in that area?

_____ What type of student body (gender, ethnic, and geographical mix) would you like to join?

_____ Do you want to go to school with your high school friends?

More Resources for Decision Making
Comparative Guide to American Colleges by James Cass and Max Birnbaum. Updated every two years.
The Fiske Guide to Colleges by Edward B. Fiske. Gives vital statistics; rates colleges in academics, social interaction, and quality of life. Provides detailed descriptions including information on degree requirements, facilities, and student activities.
Peterson's College Money Handbook. Comprehensive guide to scholarships, costs, and financial aid at U.S. colleges. Revised yearly.

College Collisions

Read the description for your character below. Spend a minute or so trying to think your way into your character. Spend several minutes with your partner, developing and intensifying the conflict before trying to reach a solution.

1. Jeff is quiet and studious. He likes to keep the room immaculately neat. He likes having the door shut so he can study without interruptions. He goes to bed at 10:00 every night and gets up at 6 a.m. in order to do calisthenics and dumbbell exercises. Getting ready for class, which includes ironing his jeans, usually takes him an hour.

Dave, Jeff's roommate, likes loud music (and has a monster stereo). He also likes lots of people. He doesn't study much, and when he's in the room he likes the door open so his friends will drop by and hang out. Dave is also a slob. He keeps most of his clothes piled on the floor around his desk. He's a night owl and often stays up till two in the morning. He has trouble waking up for his 9:30 class. On the days he makes it, he usually rolls out of bed about 9:20 and pulls on his clothes as he heads out the door.

The situation: Jeff is getting ready to go to bed. Dave breezes in, leaving the door open, and turns on the stereo. The conflict begins. To make matters worse, Dave says he wants the room to himself this Friday night so he can spend time alone with his girlfriend.

2. Janie has good intentions about studying, but lacks responsibility; she's unable to handle the freedom of college. Her workload includes psychology, calculus, French, economics, and biology.

Yulita, though not perfect, is a little more responsible. She works hard to keep up with her work as outlined by the course syllabi. She is finished with her psychology reading and just needs to review her class notes several more times.

The situation: It's Thursday night at 8:30. Janie is in her room studying for her Psych 101 mid-term, which is Friday at 2 p.m. Yulita, who is also in Psych 101, stops by to invite her to the 9:00 showing of a popular movie on campus. Janie says she has to study. Yulita tries to convince her to go and to study all day tomorrow. Janie complains that she still has 200 pages to read for Psych 101, plus a paper due in Freshman Writing that she hasn't even started. She complains that none of her profs remind her to keep up with her reading.

3. Ken is good-natured and enthusiastic. But he likes to party, which usually includes getting fall-down drunk. He has a strong personality and is very persuasive.

Anthony is a Christian. He wants to be friendly and to have friends. He also wants to please God and knows that the Bible condemns drunkenness. He likes to please people, which is often a good characteristic—but can be a problem sometimes.

The situation: It's the third Friday of the semester, 10:30 p.m. Ken invites Anthony to a party at his older brother's house. They're having a keg, Ken says, and he has invited a bunch of other guys from the dorm. If they're lucky, says Ken, his brother might even have rented some skin flicks on video. Anthony declines, but Ken keeps trying to persuade him.

4. Jill is outspoken and a self-proclaimed atheist. She believes that no intelligent person could believe in God, that Christians are superstitious and anti-intellectual, and that the Christian church has been an instrument of oppression at various times in history.

Charlene is also outspoken, but she's a Christian. She disagrees with Jill on almost every point.

The situation: It's one of those late night dorm discussions around a bowl of popcorn. The conversation has turned to the subject of Christianity and God's existence. Jill argues against God's existence and Christianity in general. Charlene disagrees and defends God's existence and the compatibility of Christianity and intelligence.

Freshman Survival Kit

Some things you should have (and use):

- alarm clock
- schedule planner
- laundry bag
- campus map

Some Suggestions

1. Registration

Make sure you know what information you need before going and take it with you. Otherwise you'll wait through long lines twice.

2. Lifestyle

College is not a rest period before "real life" begins. It *is* real life; so develop a healthy lifestyle.

a. Try to achieve balance. School is a job, so treat it that way. Work hard, but don't work all the time. You need social activities, worship, exercise, relaxation, etc.

b. Get involved in some extracurricular activities, but don't overextend. Activities are a good way to start making friends, which is the best way to get acclimated and avoid homesickness. Activities, if not overdone, can also force you to manage your time better, making you more efficient.

c. Get enough sleep. Lack of sleep and the stress of studying can make you inefficient—and a prime target for all sorts of viruses, including mononucleosis.

3. Study Habits

a. Keep up with assigned readings. Read them for the day due on the syllabus if it's noted there. Professors will not remind you, and if you get behind, things will snowball.

b. Schedule study time for each subject and stick to it. Most people who know advise students to plan on two hours of study for every hour spent in class. If you complete your assignments, work ahead (at least sometimes). Semesters generally start out slow in terms of assignments due and increase toward the end of semester, especially from midterms on.

c. The average attention span is 35-45 minutes. Then your brain needs a short break (5 minutes or less). Studying another subject for awhile can also help freshen up your mind.

d. Don't be afraid to ask for help. Many colleges and universities have free tutorial services.

4. Scheduling

a. Find your most efficient working time; study or schedule classes then. Play during your least productive hours.

b. Before settling on a semester schedule, visit a variety of classes if possible. Find professors and classes that you think you'll enjoy and that you need.

c. If you go the liberal arts route, don't put off your general education requirements until your senior year.

d. Don't take a class just because your friends are taking it; take what you need and are interested in.

Test the Spirits

1. Remember that all truth is God's truth. We can boldly seek for truth wherever it may be found.

2. Separate wheat and chaff. First Thessalonians 5:21 says, "Test everything. Hold on to the good." We must learn to evaluate the ideas we're exposed to and reject whatever isn't good. Paul praised the Berean Christians because they refused to accept his teaching at face value; they searched the Scriptures and tested Paul's message against what God had already revealed.

We need to test what we hear at church as well as what we hear at college. But we must be humble as we question, wanting to know God's truth so that we can submit to His will. Questioning authority just because we want to rebel is not truth-seeking.

3. Test philosophies. In Colossians 2:8 Paul writes, "See to it that no one takes you captive through hollow and deceptive philosophy, which depends on human tradition and the basic principles of this world rather than on Christ." One good way to test a philosophy or movement is to ask, "Where is God in this picture?" or, "Who is god in this picture?"

Satan deceived and tempted Adam and Eve with these lies: "You will not surely die" and "God knows that when you eat of it [the fruit] your eyes will be opened, and you will be like God, knowing good and evil" (Genesis 3:4, 5). Like Adam and Eve, each time we sin we reject God's way and choose ours. Many false philosophies also reject God's authority and replace it with a human one—in essence, making mankind god.

4. Remember that even professors can be wrong. Professors are learned people. Some are brilliant. Yet brilliance doesn't necessarily mean wisdom in God's eyes. Paul tells us that the "wisdom of this world is foolishness in God's sight" (I Corinthians 3:19). Brilliant though your professor may be, he or she may be teaching something that just isn't true. This doesn't mean, though, that your professor has *nothing* to teach you.

5. Ask questions. Asking questions about our beliefs is necessary and a part of growth. In fact, some struggling in our faith may even make us stronger. But we must be careful of our motives. There are two kinds of questioners: the honest, who are truly confused and want to know and submit to God's truth; and the dishonest, who use their intellectual "doubts" as a way to avoid obedience.

Suggestions for Further Reading
Developing a Christian Mind by Nancy Barcus (Inter-Varsity Press)
Mere Christianity by C.S. Lewis

What If?

At one time or another, most college students face situations like these. For each situation, ask: What if this person had Christian friends to turn to? What if this person didn't? What difference might having Christian friends make in the outcome?

1. It's Friday night. Once again Jill is without a date. Her boyfriend broke up with her five weeks ago, and she hasn't had a date since. She's beginning to wonder whether there's something wrong with her. She's hurt and depressed. She feels rejected and worthless.

2. Bob hasn't been going to church lately. He knows he should go. But he stays out late every Saturday night—and Sunday morning comes so early that he has a hard time getting up.

3. Kristen plays field hockey. She loves the sport and likes her teammates, though they're pretty wild. Every weekend one of the varsity starters throws a big party. Kristen likes to go and dance and be with her friends, but she worries about the drinking. It's only halfway through the semester and already she can tell her attitude about partying has changed. She's even started drinking, too—a little. She's not sure how long her "restraint" will last.

4. T.C. has been a Christian since he was a child, or so he thought. He's taking a course called "Problems of Contemporary Thought." It's confusing him. He's no longer sure whether the Bible is true and whether he really believes in God—or whether he just thought he did because that's what his parents and Sunday School teachers told him to believe. He also worries that even if the Bible is true, he must not be a Christian—because a "real" Christian wouldn't have such strong doubts.

5. Isabel is considering spending her Christmas break in Honduras on a mission trip with kids from her home church. She wants to go to Honduras, but also wants to be home with her family and friends. She needs someone to talk to about the trip; she needs advice.

6. Kenny likes to gossip. He knows it's wrong, and he tries to stop. But he finds so many people laughable and "idiotic" that he can't resist making fun of them. Since he is quick-witted, sharp-tongued, and a good mimic, his making fun of people is quite popular with other students.

7. Tina and her roommate are exact opposites in nearly every way. All they ever seem to do is fight, unless they're giving each other the silent treatment. It's so bad that Tina has started avoiding her own room. Her roommate wants to ask the Residence Director for permission to switch roommates with somebody else. Tina's not sure it's the right thing to do, but she's also not sure how to get along.

8. Bill has been taking an ego beating since school started. He made the JV soccer team—but has to sit on the bench the whole game unless the team is ahead by five goals. He's behind in Spanish 101 even though he took Spanish for two years in high school. To top it all off, he just flunked his first calculus exam, which is worth one fifth of his semester grade. It's the first time he ever flunked anything. He feels like a total loser—that he's definitely not college material after all.

Owen Open-Minded

"I think everybody should be open-minded. Forget what your parents taught you. If you agree with what I think, then you can be open-minded too."

Gary Granola

"We need to get back to nature and become one with our brothers and sisters the animals. If we just seek harmony with the planet, we can save it and live at peace with all beings."

Mary Missionary

"I know some people want to major in secular things like business, but I know the only right thing is to serve God full-time. I just wish I didn't have to waste all this time taking classes. All I need is a Bible and a pith helmet."

Quentin Questioner

"All these rules everybody finds in the Bible—they're not there at all. The Bible doesn't condemn keg parties or marijuana—not by name, anyway. And I'm sure if the Bible was being written today it would say that sex is okay before marriage. No doubt about it."

Ingrid Intellectual

"Christianity is actually quite interesting as a development of world religions. Like most religions, it has scriptures which it claims are divinely inspired; its members perform religious rites similar to those of most other belief systems. It's amazing how strong a hold this kind of superstition has on the uneducated, even in our modern society."

Patrick Progressive

"There is no such thing as truth. If there is, there's no way we can know it for sure. So you can't believe in Christianity. You just have to accept uncertainty and put on a happy face. Actually, it's kind of liberating. If there's no meaning, you're totally free, right?"

Ursula Utopia

"Don't bother with that baloney about eternal life. If we just house the homeless, stop racism, halt the oppression of women, teach people how to read, end the arms race, and outlaw acid rain, we'll have heaven on earth by the end of the semester."

Charlie Churchcrusher

"Christians are the biggest hypocrites in the world. They always talk about love and acceptance, but they don't accept anyone. They want everyone to be just like them. Look at the Crusades—they slaughtered people who didn't agree with them. It's the same thing all through history. They hoodwink a bunch of stupid poor people into giving them all their money and then saddle them with a bunch of rules they don't even try to keep themselves. Look at the TV evangelists!"

How to Talk to Kids about Suicide

by David E. Rice, Ph.D.

Teen suicide. The mere mention of it causes heads to turn and conversations to pause. As with E.F. Hutton, people listen when the topic is broached. Yet in many ways it is a taboo subject, still shrouded with mystery, packed with fascination—and sadly, often romanticized.

As you lead these sessions on "A Reason to Live," you'll present a positive alternative to suicide—choosing God's gift of life. In the process you'll need to deal with the subject of suicide itself, with your group and perhaps with troubled individuals as well. That may not be easy, but it is vital.

Why We Must Talk

Why is it difficult for youth workers to talk about teen suicide?

At first, not many know what to say. They fear asking the wrong question, one that will touch a nerve that could set off an angry explosion or plunge a teenager further into the suicidal depths. Many potentially suicidal teenagers have been passed by because an adult was too uncomfortable and uncertain with words and feelings to even approach them.

Second, adults tend to downplay adolescent problems. After all, kids are in the prime of life, aren't they? What do they have to worry about? As a result, young people can feel demeaned, belittled, and isolated, holding their pain and sadness deep inside instead of getting the relief a caring and interested adult could bring.

Third, peers and adults alike can feel impotent when faced with a suicidal youngster. They think, *I can't help or stop this thing from happening.* They feel powerless and paralyzed. But the fact is that it's the suicidal boy or girl who feels the most hopeless of all.

Fourth, many people don't recognize the signs and symptoms. "He's just going through a phase," or, "She's always talking like that," are statements often made about suicidal teens. Because suicidal ideas, feelings, and intent can be mixed in with the normal highs and lows of adolescence, a student at risk can be overlooked and written off as just "being a typical teenager."

As youth workers we cannot afford to sit back on our hands or bite our lips and look the other way, hoping the problem will go away. Teens in the U.S. are killing themselves at an alarming rate triple that of the 1950s. It is estimated that there is one teen suicide every 90 minutes—14 a day, 5,000 per year. For every suicide, it is estimated, there are 50 to 100 attempts. That works out to about 80 attempts each hour. By the time you finish reading this article, perhaps 20 teens will have attempted to take their lives.

Suicide Myths

Many youth workers are hampered by myths about suicide. Francine Klagsbrun, in her book *Too Young To Die*, says one of the most widespread fallacies is that people who talk about killing themselves never do. Believing that myth can lead us to ignore the chatter and avoid taking action. In reality, those who threaten suicide often have serious thoughts and plans. Their warnings are clues that they need help.

Another myth Klagsbrun cites: Once a teen has attempted suicide, the shame and guilt will keep him or her from trying again. In fact, once kids have crossed the line, it can actually become easier to try again if the conditions in their lives do not change. It is estimated that of every five suicides, four were preceded by multiple attempts.

A third myth holds that those who have come out of a depression, seemingly improved, no longer feel suicidal. The reverse can be true; some appear calm and relaxed because they have made the decision to end their lives. Others, beginning to feel better, kill themselves because they have the energy to do it.

A fourth myth: "Nothing could have stopped him once he decided to end his life." In reality, suicidal people have mixed feelings about their intentions. Many suicides can be prevented if we can find that vein of desire to live.

A fifth myth states that suicides are always accompanied by a note. On the contrary, only 15% of people who kill themselves leave a note. It's felt that a high number of "accidental" teen deaths were actually suicides, but the absence of notes leads authorities to label them otherwise.

A sixth myth that most suicides occur at night or in bad weather can cause us to miss important clues. More teen suicides occur between 3:00 and 6:00 in the evening, when kids come home from school, than late at night. Suicide rates also go up during the spring months, reaching a peak in April and May; they decrease during December and January.

Still another myth is that mentioning suicide gives teens the idea to commit it. We fear they'll think, *Oh, thanks for the idea. I've never thought of that before.* Instead, bringing up the topic can be a relief, not permission. It's saying to the young person, "It's okay to talk to me about it. I can handle it."

Why Suicide?

Understanding why kids kill themselves can give you a better feeling of control if you encounter a suicidal young person.

Almost all suicidal people seem to have mixed feelings: wanting to die versus wanting to live; feeling hopeless, yet hoping for a last minute solution; wanting to pull away from loved ones and friends, yet needing to communicate and move closer to them.

Suicide is an act that communicates. It begs for someone to notice the feelings of sadness, hopelessness, loss, isolation, self-criticism, and overwhelming impotence. It is a message often aimed at specific family members or friends. It serves as a vehicle to get across a point when all other forms of expression have broken down. If you are faced with a potential suicide, ask yourself, "What is this person trying to say, and who is the statement aimed at?"

Watching Your Group

How can you help prevent suicide among your young people?

First, be a good observer of your kids. Watch for losses in their lives—family breakup, death, end of a romance or loss of a job, poor grades, or being cut from a team. Suicide begins with a loss and subsequent feelings of helplessness, hopelessness, and despair. Life at this point can feel too overwhelming to move another inch.

When you see a problem, approach the teen with what you observe. Stating your concern as an observation can help him or her feel you aren't being critical and intrusive—just observant and caring. For example, let's say you notice that Todd, a group member, has been isolating himself. You approach him and say, "Todd, I've noticed over the past several weeks that you've gotten quieter and quieter. I'm concerned about you. Is there anything

you'd like to talk to me about, or any problem I can help you with?" This gives the boy emotional room to move, yet lets him know someone is checking on him in love.

Listen for direct threats and words of warning such as, "I wish I weren't here," "I want to be dead," or, "I have nothing to live for." Or a friend may hear statements like these and report them to you. If so, approach the troubled adolescent with what you've heard. This tells him or her that the message is being heard by people who care.

Other signs to look for: Heavy drinking; drug use; acts of delinquency or violence; mood changes that seem to involve increasing depression; withdrawal; apathy; self-criticism; previous suicide threats or attempts; a family history of alcohol or drug abuse, sexual molestation, or physical beatings.

It's important to tell others when you suspect a person is suicidal. Talk to significant people in the youngster's life—parents, counselors, ministers, close friends, teachers, coaches—and get their input. They need to be told, should be involved, and can help. Even if you have to break a confidence, do so. Your priority is to save a life—even at the expense of your friendship with the young person if necessary.

Taking Action

If you counsel a suicidal teen, don't be afraid to ask questions like, "Are you thinking of hurting yourself?" or, "Do you want to kill yourself?" If the answer is yes, ask, "How long have you thought about killing yourself?" and "What is your plan to kill yourself?" Remember, asking these questions is not putting the idea in the person's mind. You're saying that you are picking up on the clues and taking notice.

Show the young person you understand and sympathize. Don't give pat answers such as, "It'll be all right tomorrow," or, "There's nothing to worry about." He or she needs to know you want to understand; it gives a sense that he or she isn't so isolated and different.

If the person claims, "You don't know what I'm feeling," agree. Say, "Tell me more, then. I really want to know." Don't label the teen's feelings as silly, exaggerated, or blown out of proportion, which would isolate him or her even further.

If you fear the teen is in imminent danger, don't leave him or her. Stay until help comes or the immediate crisis passes. The teen may fight you on this, but stick with him or her anyway. Don't be afraid to call for emergency help.

Ask the teen's parents to rid their home of any

dangerous objects such as guns, razor blades, ropes, poisons, alcohol, and medications. They should not leave the youth alone even it it means taking time off work or cancelling important engagements.

Push the parents to seek professional help—from a therapist comfortable with young people in general and with suicidal teens in particular. He or she must be someone the adolescent and family members can relate to and trust. Call other youth workers or the suicide prevention center in your area for possible referrals. Check to see whether the teen is or was in therapy and call that therapist.

Few things grab us in the gut like suicidal statements and gestures. Yet overcoming our discomfort in talking about the subject can be the biggest step toward preventing suicides among young people. When it comes to providing a reason to live, youth workers like you are often the first line of defense.

Dr. David E. Rice is a licensed therapist with South Coast Psychological Center in Irvine, California. A former junior high teacher and youth pastor, he travels nationwide conducting a seminar called "Understanding Your Teenager" for parents. Author of Parents In Control *(Harvest House Publishers), Dave also writes for* Christian Parenting Today *magazine and* Parents and Teens *newsletter.*

A Reason to Live

by Marion Duckworth

Marion Duckworth is the author of several books, including *Why Teens Are Killing Themselves and What You Can Do about It* (Here's Life Publishers). She has spoken to church groups on the subjects of teen suicide and self-image, and has taught young people in Sunday School. A former pastor's wife, she has worked with youth groups—and raised three teenagers.

"Are you kidding? Kids have every reason to live."

That may be true, but in recent years suicide has been the second leading cause of death among U.S. teenagers. And every year at least 500,000 young people attempt to take their own lives in the U.S. About 5,000 succeed.

It's possible that there are deeply troubled kids like these in your church. Even if there aren't, your kids may know friends who are desperate and would accept a peer's help. And in times like ours, every young person needs a good reason to look at life with hopeful eyes.

In this session you'll discuss situations that can make kids feel desperate. Then you'll talk about how to keep from making impulsive, destructive decisions—the kind that lead to the tragedy of suicide.

Temporary
Problem,
Permanent
Solution

The Point	To inform teens of circumstances which tend to prompt suicide, and, using biblical principles, to help them realize there are always alternatives for solving problems with God's help.
The Passages	Job 6:1-17; 7:11; Psalm 38
The Preparation	You'll need the following: • Bibles • Pencils • Copies of "On the Edge" (Student Sheet 19) • Copies of "The Big Picture" (Student Sheet 20)

Be Reasonable

Seeing the Danger of Making Impulsive, Extreme Decisions

Read or tell the following story:

Eddie had a problem. He'd just gotten a terrible haircut. He knew there was only one thing to do: He ran home and shaved his head!

Then his car broke down for the third time that month. There was only one thing to do—so he pushed it over the bank into the river!

That afternoon he had another problem: He got a "D" on his first test in geometry. Once again, he knew there was only one thing to do: Drop geometry, even though he needed it to get into college, and take home ec instead!

That night Eddie had one more problem. He wanted to be a musician, but in his first public appearance with a group, he was so nervous that he played a wrong chord on his guitar. As usual, there was only one thing to do: Quit the group and vow never to play in public again!

What's wrong with Eddie? (He overreacts; he makes extreme, impulsive decisions that only make things worse; he thinks there's only one solution to every problem.)

What could Eddie have done instead of shaving his head, trashing his car, etc.? (Wear a hat; sell the car; get a geometry tutor; keep practicing, etc.)

Why do people choose extreme "solutions" as Eddie did? (They're angry, embarrased, or upset.)

Have you ever felt that way and made a decision you regretted? Be ready to share an experience of your own.

You were able to come up with more reasonable solutions than Eddie did because you weren't emotionally involved in his situation. Sometimes people who have a temporary problem make the mistake of picking a permanent solution. The results can be a lot worse than having to walk around with a shaved head. Today we're going to talk about one of the most permanent, extreme decisions of all.

Tragic Choices

Learning Facts about Teen Suicide

You've probably heard of young people who have decided to "solve" their problems by committing suicide. In recent years it's been the second leading cause of death among teenagers. Every year in the U.S. more than 5,000 young people end their lives. Every year at least half a million kids attempt suicide.

There are a lot of misunderstandings floating around about the subject of suicide. Since it's so important, let's take a true-false quiz to see how much we know about it.

1. Kids who are suicidal mostly live in poverty.

(False. More of them come from middle and upper middle class families.)

2. Kids who go to Christian churches hardly ever attempt suicide, much less take their own lives.

(False. Surveys show that it happens in families that attend church as well as those that do not.)

3. Suicidal people are not usually crazy.

(True. They are not usually psychotic, which is the medical term for the common expression, "crazy.")

4. Three main reasons why young people attempt suicide: They want to

escape a situation they can't stand, show others how miserable they are, or punish themselves or someone else.

(True.)

5. If you live in a small town you won't meet any suicidal kids; it only happens in big cities.

(False. It happens in all kinds of places.)

6. Only a certain type of kid attempts suicide—the kind who is very quiet and doesn't have any friends.

(False. A number of them fit that category, but some are outgoing and have lots of friends.)

7. Kids who are suicidal usually don't want to die; they just want to find a way out of their situation.

(True. They want to live, but feel things are hopeless, that there are no answers to their problems.)

8. Young people who have been suicidal say later that one thing they wanted most was someone to listen to them.

(True.)

How did you do on the quiz? Which answers most surprised you?

Tell Me Why
Exploring Reasons Why Kids Become Suicidal

Distribute Student Sheet 19, "On the Edge." Have volunteers read the true stories aloud. Stop after each story and discuss reasons why the person became suicidal. Here are some possibilities:

1. (Dave couldn't please his parents; he had no friends; he was used to taking drugs to escape.)

2. (Kent was shy, found it hard to mix, and felt "different.")

3. (Sonia was angry over losing family relationships; she had a poor relationship with her boyfriend; she may have been influenced by music.)

4. (Ben was angry over the loss of his dad; he had a poor relationship with his mom, used alcohol, and had trouble with his girlfriend.)

What other events or emotions might influence a person to feel suicidal? (A loss—of a close friend or relative, faith, reputation, health, status, something he or she loved; unrealistic expectations, lack of self-worth, lack of satisfactory relationships, sense of inadequacy; physical reasons such as a chemical imbalance.)

Be sure kids understand that there's usually more than one reason why a person feels suicidal. Ben, for instance, missed his father and had a poor relationship with his mother—and used alcohol. Then something happened that seemed to be the "last straw"—the argument with his girlfriend.

Down but Definitely Not Out
Discovering How Bible Characters Handled Depression

Most suicidal kids are depressed. This is more than the occasional "down" feeling we all experience. Severely depressed people feel flattened, pressed down, so that hope is squeezed out of them. They feel life is no good and never will be, and that feeling is there day after day. As far as they can see, there's nothing they can do to change it.

Life was like that for some people in the Bible, too.

Divide the group into two teams; the first will "interview" Job by reading Job 6:1-17; 7:11. The second will "interview" David by reading Psalm 38.

Have kids look for answers to the following questions:

What words describe this person's feelings?

How does this person express his feelings of aloneness?

Then regather and discuss:

Job had been a healthy, rich man and had a happy family. Then he got sick, lost all his possessions and all his family except his wife. What words describe how he felt? (Job 6:1, 2, 4: He had so much anguish it seemed to weigh more than all the sand in the world; he felt God had shot him full of arrows; he felt poisoned and terrified.)

What words describe how David felt? (Psalm 38: 2-4, 7, 8: He felt as though God had shot him with arrows; he felt guilty, weak, in pain, sick, feeble, and crushed.)

How did Job's situation make him feel about living? (Job 6:8, 9: He wished he were dead.)

How did David show the way he felt? (Psalm 38:6, 8: He was bowed down and went around mourning all day; he groaned and sighed.)

How did Job feel about his friends? (Job 6:14-17: He felt he couldn't depend on them.)

How about David's friends? (Psalm 38:11-14: His friends avoided him and even turned against him. He didn't even try to talk to them.)

Did Job hide in his room and suffer alone? (Job 7:11: No. He talked and even complained about his feelings.)

David didn't keep his feelings to himself either. To whom did he go? (Psalm 38:9, 21, 22: He went to God.)

Getting flattened by problems happens to everybody. As Job and David show, one important thing to remember is not to keep our feelings inside.

Be sure to emphasize that anyone who is depressed for more than two weeks or so should go to an understanding adult who has the experience and training to help.

Gaining Perspective
Helping Students See the Big Picture

Have students complete Student Sheet 20, "The Big Picture," individually. When they're done, discuss their answers to the two questions on the sheet.

It helps to see the "big picture" in real life. When we focus too tightly on a problem, we can't see all the solutions available.

How did Job and David see a "bigger picture"? (They remembered that God was there and talked to Him; they expressed their feelings by talking or writing them down.)

Is it hard or easy to say how you feel?

How do you let your emotions out?

What's your favorite way to put your problem in words—write in a journal, write a poem, tell someone, or write a letter?

Next time you face a big problem, how could you see the big picture? (Do something to calm down; write your problem out in one sentence; tell someone about it; read about people in the Bible who had problems to assure yourself you're not weird; talk to God about your problem they way David did.)

God can help calm us down and broaden our perspective. Then we can

see not only the problem, but some sensible solutions, too.

Have one student read Psalm 38:21, 22 and another Psalm 40:17.

When life squashed him, David told God about it in prayer and asked for help. Ask kids to list David's requests and the names he uses for God (Lord, Savior, deliverer). Close by leading the group in a prayer based on these passages.

How much is a human life worth? Not much by itself, it would seem from these statements:

"You've got to make something of yourself."

"That guy must be worth a couple million."

"Humans like to think they're something special, but there are plenty of other planets in the universe."

"It's my life; I can end it when and how I choose."

The idea that a human being is important because he or she has been created by God—that seems old-fashioned these days. When kids are told that they are only higher animals, that they have the right to do with their bodies as they please, that the quality of their lives is more important than living, it's no surprise that some might think it okay to end their own lives. That's why this session emphasizes how God values—and owns—each of us.

God's View of Suicide

The Point

To present a biblical view of the value of life; to show that suicide is wrong; and to help teens understand how this should affect the way they see themselves and others.

The Passages

Genesis 1:27; 5:1; Exodus 20:13; Leviticus 24:17; Psalm 8; 139:13-16; Matthew 6:26; 12:12a; Romans 5:5-8; Ephesians 1:4

The Preparation

You'll need the following:
• Bibles
• Copies of "Moving Day" (Student Sheet 21)
• Copies of "Alignment Time" (Student Sheet 22)
• Pencils
• Newsprint and marker or chalkboard and chalk
• Small prizes (optional)

Big Bucks
Talking about the Value of Things

Divide the group into two teams. Explain that you're going to describe for each team an item that was auctioned off in a particular year. The team will have 20 seconds to confer and decide on the value of its item. In each round, the team with the closest guess wins the point.

Round 1

Team A: **In 1978, Joan Crawford's false eyelashes.** ($325)

Team B: **In 1975, a platinum disc presented to John Lennon for the album *Rock and Roll.*** ($7,700)

Round 2

Team A: **In 1978, a copy of the first book ever printed by movable type—the Bible.** ($2 million)

Team B: **In 1979, an autograph of Button Gwinnett, one of the signers of the Declaration of Independence.** ($100,000)

Round 3

Team A: **In 1970, a hat worn by Napoleon.** ($29,471)

Team B: **In 1980, a cup made in China in the 15th century.** ($1 million)

Round 4

Team A: **In 1980, an original painting of Samson and Delilah by Rubens.** ($5.4 million)

Team B: **In 1980, a poster by Toulouse-Lautrec titled "Moulin Rouge."** ($52,000)

Round 5

Team A: **In 1979, a 1936 Mercedes-Benz roadster.** ($421,040)

Team B: **In 1981, a letter handwritten by Ronald Reagan about Frank Sinatra.** ($12,500)

(Sources: *Auction Madness,* Charles Hamilton, Everest House Publishers, 1981; *The Book of Lists #3,* Amy Wallace, David Wallechinsky, and Irving Wallace, William Morrow and Company, Inc., 1983.)

If you wish, give small prizes to the winning team. Point out that knowing the real value of an item can make a big difference.

What Do You Prize?
Deciding What's Most Important to Us

Why were those auctioned-off items so valuable? (They were rare, part of an important event in the past, or belonged to a well-known person.)

Let's see what standards you use to decide what's valuable. Pass out copies of "Moving Day" (Student Sheet 21) and have kids work individually, deciding which item is most valuable to them, which is number two, etc. When they are finished, ask them to share and explain their choices. Did they have trouble deciding on their priorities?

Things are often most valuable to us when they're tied in with someone we love. Things that we made ourselves, that symbolize something about us, or that show our accomplishments are also important to us.

What's the most important thing you own? Why?

Step 3

Solving the Case
Discovering God's Value System

God has a value system, too. We're going to look for clues in God's Word that show what in this world is most important to Him. Believe it or not, the answer has a lot to do with you.

Assign each of the following seven passages to individuals or teams. Each person or team should find a clue to what God thinks is most valuable. List these on chalkboard or newsprint when you regather and discuss. As needed, use the additional information in your discussion.

1. *Genesis 1:27; 5:1*—(Clue: People are made in God's image, and are set apart as special to Him because they can be friends with Him.)

God created fish, birds, and all other animals, but no mention is made anywhere that they are created in God's image. That privilege is reserved only for people. A person has a spirit, and God is Spirit. That alikeness means that people are the only creatures who can know God intimately.

2. *Exodus 20:13; Leviticus 24:17*—(Clue: Our lives come from God, and only He has a right to take them.)

We're not to murder someone else—or to kill ourselves. We can't do as we please with something that doesn't belong to us. The family car, the money in mom's wallet, the things in a teacher's drawer—they don't belong to us, so we can't trash them. Our lives belong to the Creator of life.

Six people in Scripture did take their own lives. They were Zimri, Ahithophel, Abimelech, Saul, Samson, and Judas (I Kings 16:18; II Samuel 17:23; Judges 9:53, 54; I Samuel 31:4, 5; I Chronicles 10:4, 5; Judges 16:25-30; Matthew 27:5; Acts 1:18). But nowhere does God condone what they did. The Bible tells us about a lot of behavior—including murder, thievery, and lying. That doesn't mean God thinks they're okay.

3. *Psalm 8*—(Clue: We may seem insignificant, but God cares for us and has honored us with a special role in overseeing what He has created.)

Think about how big the universe is. Then think about the fact that God places such value on us even though we're so tiny in comparison! God has given us major responsibilities in caring for the earth as His representatives.

4. *Matthew 6:26; 12:12*—(Clue: Jesus said people are more important to God than are other earthly living things.)

We are more valuable than birds and sheep, Jesus said. They're only two examples. This doesn't mean we should mistreat animals, but it does indicate that we're in a class by ourselves.

5. *Psalm 139:7-12*—(Clue: God carefully supervised our individual creation and made us wonderful; each day of our lives is His gift.)

What does God value most in His creation? Not the biggest diamond or the richest gold mine. It's us! Some of us may have been told that we're unwanted, but that's not true. God wanted you. He created your spirit so you could communicate with Him. He "knit" you as only He could. We honor Him by appreciating ourselves and seeing our bodies as a gift. Verse 16 points out that our life span is determined by God, not by us.

6. *Romans 5:5-8*—(Clue: God loves us, sacrificed His Son for us, and wants to live in us.)

The item we value most is the one we love most. We keep it in a special place and do everything we can to preserve it. If we catch anyone misusing it, we're ready to do battle. It's set apart in our minds from all the other stuff we have. We're like that to God. He doesn't just love us a little bit; He's poured out His love into our hearts through the Holy Spirit, who comes to live in us if we've received His Son. Because God loves us, He sent Christ to die in our place. God values us enough to want us to live with Him forever.

Making Our Case
Showing That Human Life Is Sacred

Let's say someone challenges you with this statement: "If life seems totally pointless and miserable to a person, he or she has the right to end it all." Using the passages we just studied, how could you answer?

Give kids a few minutes to summarize the principles they found in the verses. Write the result as a statement on the board or newsprint. It might go something like this:

God values humans most. We are created in God's image. He chose us to live with Him forever and made it possible by sacrificing His Son. He comes to live in us. Our lives belong to God and not to ourselves. We are forbidden to murder, and suicide is self-murder. God participates in the creation of every individual and determines the length of his or her life.

How could all of this help someone who doesn't feel life is worth living? Listen to kids' opinions. Point out that the ban on taking a life might make the person think twice about suicide, but he or she might be more impressed by the possibility that life could become more meaningful if God loves and values him or her.

Line Up!
Aligning Our Self-worth with God's View

Distribute copies of "Alignment Time" (Student Sheet 22). Let group members evaluate themselves and answer the questions. Don't press anyone to share the results. Then comment:

When we feel worthless or feel that no one cares, it's a signal that our thinking needs realignment. The way to line our thinking up with God's is to keep reflecting on what He says is true about us. If we're Christians, we can ask the Holy Spirit to remind us and to help change the way we see ourselves. That's also true of the way we see others. No matter how a person seems to us—threatening or strange or a "loser"—he or she is valuable to God.

Close with silent prayer, giving kids a chance to talk to God about their reactions to this session.

You've probably seen the scene many times on TV—sometimes played for laughs. A despondent character teeters on the ledge of a tall building, threatening to jump. At the window another character tries to talk the first into coming back inside.

"There's nothing to live for," the would-be jumper cries.

"Oh, yes, there is," the other character replies, doing his or her best to come up with a list of reasons to go on living.

What would you say in a situation like that? Life is difficult, after all—and no less so for teenagers. Are there joys and challenges that make living worthwhile? Is there a more "abundant life" available to Christian kids?

This session affirms the adventure that living can be. Use it to remind your young people that in spite of pain, God offers a richly satisfying life for them to enjoy.

Reasons to Live

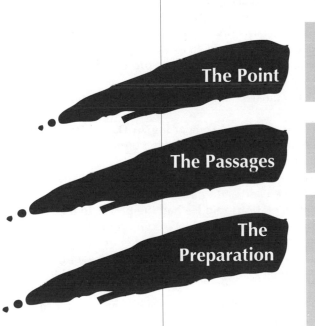

The Point

To help kids realize that, although life can be disappointing and difficult, God cares about the quality of their lives; and to remind kids that life can be fulfilling and even fun.

The Passages

Ecclesiastes 3:1, 4, 12, 13; John 14:15-18, 25, 26; 10:10; 16:33; I Timothy 6:17

The Preparation

You'll need the following:
• Bibles
• Pens or pencils
• "A Day to Forget" (Student Sheet 23)
• "Jim's Story" (Student Sheet 24)
• Equipment for games that you choose for Step 5 (optional)

A Day to Forget
Discussing Frustrating Experiences

Distribute "A Day to Forget" (Student Sheet 23). Ask kids to fill in the emotions they'd feel in each situation. Discuss times when students have had days like that and how they felt.

Did the words you used get stronger with each negative experience? Why?

What words describe how you might feel after the last incident?

When one bad thing happens on top of another, frustration can build up and make us feel as though all the fun has gone out of life. Observe that some problems are a lot worse than the ones on the sheet and can make us feel badly for a longer time. Ask kids to think of some examples. As needed, mention a few—serious illness, divorce, death in the family, etc.

When a lot of hard things happen to you, what colors best represent the way you see life?

What color would you like your life to be?

This Way Out and Up
Discovering That God Is There to Help

Ask individuals or teams to look up the passages that follow. Read the true/false statements one at a time; the person or team with the corresponding passage should decide whether the statement is true and explain why. As needed, supplement kids' comments with the information and questions provided.

1. *Ecclesiastes 3:1, 4.* **When something goes wrong, it means life is rotten and will never be any better.** (False.)

It's normal to be sad sometimes and happy sometimes. Life is like riding down a strange road with a lot of sharp curves and potholes. We wish they weren't there, but wishing doesn't make them go away.

2. *John 16:33* (first two sentences). **Christians are protected from having problems.** (False.)

Even Jesus, who was perfect, had problems. People misunderstood and even wanted to kill Him.

Why do things go wrong in our lives? Look at the "A Day to Forget" list and tell me why things like that happen. (We often don't know in individual cases. But we live in an imperfect, fallen world. Things break, there is sickness and death, people are selfish, we make mistakes. Sin is in the world and will be until Jesus creates a new heaven and earth that are perfect.)

3. *John 16:33* (third sentence). **Jesus said He had the power to do something about the way things are in this world.** (True.)

What does "overcome" mean? (Conquer, get the better of.) That means we don't have to live like victims who can't do anything when irritating things happen. God can give us the strength and patience to handle them and to eventually enjoy life again.

4. *John 14:15-18, 25, 26.* **Jesus is in heaven, so we just have to try to guess what He'd do in our situation.** (False.)

Christ sent the Holy Spirit to live in Christians. The Spirit teaches us many things, including how to cope with life's hard times. The ability to cope is in us because, if we're believers, God is in us.

How long will He help us? (Forever.)

But what if we feel as if we're totally alone? (Count on the truth as expressed in God's Word. An illustration: We may feel broke, but if we look at our bankbook and see the $300 we saved last summer, we know we're not.)

How will the Holy Spirit help us? By miraculously fixing our broken zippers? (By teaching us all things and reminding us what Jesus said. He'll show us ways to cope that we wouldn't have thought of on our own.)

5. *John 10:10.* **Jesus wants to help us have a full life.** (True.)

Another word for "full" is "complete." Illustrate by asking what students collect (baseball cards, one musician's tapes or records, etc.) and whether they have a complete set.

One way God has enabled us to live a full life is by being with us all the time. We were created to live as His friends, to tell Him all about our lives every day and trust Him to help us get out of the "potholes." It's being friends with God that makes us complete.

6. *I Timothy 6:17b.* **Christians who expect to have fun aren't very spiritual.** (False.)

God means for us to be happy and enjoy life. There is work He wants us to do, and sacrifices we may need to make. But He didn't create us to be miserable. He created us to have satisfying lives.

Read Ecclesiastes 3:12, 13. **Where does happiness come from?** (It's a gift of God.)

What are three sources of happiness listed here? (Doing good, eating and drinking [which probably represents a variety of everyday activities], and enjoying work.)

How do you feel when you do something good for another person?

Besides eating and drinking, what other everyday activities can be enjoyable gifts from God? (Relating to family members; working on hobbies; being with friends, etc.)

How can even school and work make us happy? (By giving us the satisfaction of doing our best, achieving goals, acquiring new skills, etc.)

The Gift Shop
Seeing God-given Abilities That Help Make Life Rewarding

What's one thing you did last week that you really enjoyed?

Listen to responses. After each answer, ask what God-given abilities were used in that activity. List these gifts on the board. (Examples: Creativity, intelligence, sense of humor, laughter, physical strength or skill, any of the five senses, musical or artistic talent, ability to relate to friends, etc.)

What if God had made sunsets but not eyes? Or flowers but no noses? (We wouldn't be able to enjoy what He'd made. People with certain disabilities can't enjoy everything, but most can appreciate many things.)

God has given us so much to see, hear, think about, and do—plus most of the abilities to go with them. What does that tell you about God? (One possibility: That He cares whether we enjoy life.)

Before moving to the next step, pause briefly for silent prayer. Encourage kids to thank God for one ability or example of natural beauty they've enjoyed recently.

Jim's Story
Discovering How Life Can Become Meaningful Again

Distribute Student Sheet 24, "Jim's story." When students have had time to read and fill it out, discuss their responses. You may want to refer to these suggested steps:

1. It's hard to be made fun of, and Jim has probably kept his feelings pretty much to himself. The first thing he needs to do is talk to a sympathetic adult about his feelings of inferiority and hopelessness.

2. Jim could learn a special skill to give him confidence. If he likes to write, maybe he could work on the school paper; if he's into music, maybe he could play in the band.

3. Jim doesn't have to spend all his time with the unkind "friend." He can look for new friends, too, especially others who need friends. He could ask a counselor or other caring adult to help him develop friendship-making skills.

4. Jim probably doesn't realize how important he is to God—that God accepts and loves him. He needs to join a group of Christian kids who show God's love through their actions as well as their words.

5. Getting involved in projects that help others would be a good idea for Jim. He'd probably spend less time worrying about himself and make friends at the same time.

When we exercise the abilities God has given us, life becomes more satisfying and rewarding. Jesus Christ invites you to have life "to the full" His way (John 10:10).

(Note: You may want to invite those who've never done so to talk with you about receiving Christ.)

Celebrating Life (optional)
Demonstrating That Life Can Be Fun

If possible, take time just to have some fun. Choose from the activities that follow, or provide your own. Emphasize enjoyment of the game(s) rather than winning or losing.

1. Seat two pairs of blindfolded volunteers in front. One member of each pair must shell a peanut and feed it to the other. The pair that finishes first wins.

2. Form two teams. One person from Team A stands before Team B and whistles "Yankee Doodle." Team B does all it can in ten seconds (except touching) to make the whistler laugh. If the whistler stops whistling, he or she is disqualified. Then have someone from Team B whistle for Team A, etc.

3. Form two teams. Have all kids take off their shoes. Toss the shoes into a pile in the center of the room. At your signal, everyone retrieves his or her shoes and puts them on. The team that finishes first wins.

When the games are over, review the God-given abilities that each game used.

"I couldn't see any way out."

That's what a lot of kids who've survived suicide attempts say they were thinking just before they hurt themselves. But there are "ways out"—whatever the circumstances.

This session is designed to help students avoid painting themselves into an emotional corner. It also provides help for those who feel hopelessly trapped and unable to hold on any longer.

No Way Out?

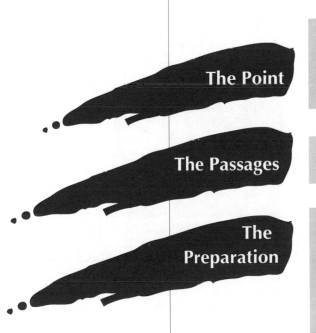

The Point

To help kids identify situations in which they could feel trapped now or in the future, and to help them recognize how God and people can help in those circumstances.

The Passages

Exodus 14:5-31; Acts 16:16-34; I Corinthians 10:13; Hebrews 2:8

The Preparation

You'll need the following:
• Bibles
• Pens or pencils
• "Trapped!" (Student Sheet 25)
• "No Way Out?" (Student Sheet 26)
• Small prizes (optional)
• Chalkboard and chalk or newsprint and marker

Name That Trap
Thinking about Traps

I'll give you someone's name, and you tell me who or what trapped that person. If desired, use more current examples. You could form teams, award a point for each right answer, and give prizes to the winners.

   l. Daniel (King Darius, in the lions' den.)
   2. Anne Frank (The Nazis.)
   3. Richard Nixon (Watergate.)
   4. Karen Carpenter (Anorexia.)
   5. Ted Bundy (Pornography—and the police.)
   6. Samson (Delilah.)
   7. John Belushi (Drugs.)
   8. Pete Rose (Gambling.)

Did these people all deserve to be trapped? (No.)
How did they react to being trapped? (Daniel prayed and trusted God; Anne Frank wrote about the experience in a diary; Richard Nixon resigned; singer Karen Carpenter apparently died from the effects of self-starvation; comedian John Belushi died of a drug overdose; serial killer Ted Bundy tried to avoid prison but was eventually convicted and executed; Samson killed himself; Pete Rose was banned from baseball.)

What's the worst trap you've ever been in or heard of? Why was it so hard to escape?

A trap is a device for catching an animal, but it can also be someone or something that ensnares a person. That's the kind of trap we're going to talk about today.

Here's the Story
Focusing on Real-life Problems That Trap Kids

Distribute copies of "Trapped!" (Student Sheet 25). Give kids a minute or two to read it.

How would you advise these people if they were your friends? We're not going to respond until the end of the session, after we've had a chance to investigate what the Bible says on the subject. But you'll need to keep their stories in mind.

Ask kids to comment on how tough they think the problems in the case studies are. Then move to the next step.

How They Did It
Learning from Bible Characters Who Were Trapped

Form two or more groups. Assign one of the following Scripture passages to each: Exodus 14:5-31 and Acts 16:16-34. Ask kids to look for answers to the following three questions:

   l. Who was trapped and why?
   2. What words help you know how they must have felt?
   3. How did God help them get out of the trap?

Use the following as a discussion guide when the group regathers.
Who was trapped in Exodus 14? (The Israelites.)

Why? (Pharaoh had changed his mind about their leaving. His army was chasing them from behind and the Red Sea was in front of them.)

What about the Acts passage? (Paul and Silas were in prison because they'd preached about Jesus.)

Were Paul and Silas trapped because they were disobeying God? (No, they were obeying God. We don't always get trapped because we've done something wrong.)

How did the Israelites feel? (Terrified. They cried out to God. They wanted to go back to Egypt and be slaves again.)

What about Paul and Silas? (If they were afraid, it doesn't say. But they were severely beaten with a whip and thrown into prison, so they must have been in physical pain.)

Nevertheless, what did they do? (Have someone read Acts 16:25)

Why do you suppose the Israelites fell apart and Paul and Silas didn't? (Trusting God to help them was pretty new to Israel. Paul and Silas had God's Spirit living in them; they knew people who had been Jesus' friends while He was on earth; they had more firsthand experience with answered prayer.)

How did the Israelites get out of the trap? (God worked through Moses and rolled back the sea.)

How did Paul and Silas get out of their trap? (Through an earthquake.)

How did Israel's deliverance affect them? (Their faith grew stronger.)

How did the rescue of Paul and Silas affect the jailer? (He and his family became Christians.)

Summarize by asking the following questions:

Are traps always our fault? (Not necessarily.)

How can we expect to feel when we're trapped? (Scared, wanting to take the easy way out.)

How can we have the kind of faith Paul and Silas did? (Pray about things regularly so we're used to trusting God, instead of waiting for a major crisis; be willing to thank God, even sing to Him, when things are difficult.)

How can we expect God to help us? (He uses a variety of ways. Seldom is it through what we'd call a miracle; usually He works through a person as He did with Moses.)

If we trust God in a crisis, what effect can that have on other people? (They can see God's power; they may want to trust Him, too.)

Trap Doors
Identifying Potential Crises and Promises to Count On

Distribute Student Sheet 26, "No Way Out?" After kids have filled out Part I, discuss which traps they can and can't avoid. Let kids explain their opinions, which may differ from one another.

A trap is designed to render us helpless. Some people, when they feel helpless and hopeless, become suicidal. But we aren't helpless or hopeless, according to God's promises.

Read the three verses from Part II of the sheet. Ask kids to complete the sentence, "I am not helpless because . . . " based on the three verses. Here are suggested answers:

Mark 14:38: ("I am not helpless because I can watch [be on the lookout for temptation] and pray for God's help to avoid traps.")

I Corinthians 10:13: ("I am not helpless because God will show me a way of escape, a way to avoid a trap or stand up to the pressure.")

Hebrews 2:18: ("I am not helpless because Christ understands what it's like to be trapped, and He is able to help.")

Who's Who
Finding People to See when We Feel Trapped and Helpless

God used Moses to rescue the Israelites. He usually uses people to help people. If we want help, most of the time we have to ask for it.

If you felt trapped, what kind of person would you want to talk to? (Patient, understanding, godly, not condemning, experienced, etc.)

What kind of help could you expect? (Help to discover what your options are; to set up a plan of action; to pray for and with you; to go with you as moral support if you have to do something hard.)

What if you ask for help and the person doesn't respond? (Go to someone else.)

As a group, brainstorm a list of people to whom kids could go when they feel trapped. Write the list on the board or newsprint. The list might include parents, other mature family members, pastor, youth leader, Sunday School teacher, school teacher, school or other counselor, and adult friend.

Going to one of these people may seem too hard. What could make it easier? (A friend could arrange a meeting or go with us; the request could be made in a note instead of in person, etc.)

I've Got This Friend . . .
Answering Dilemmas with Principles Learned

Call attention again to Student Sheet 25, "Trapped!" Ask kids how they'd advise friends whose situations are described on the sheet. As needed, add the following suggestions:

1. You could help her find a shelter for pregnant women. Call the Salvation Army or ask a responsible adult who might know of a shelter. You can also ask your pastor to act as a go-between for her and her family.

2. Invite him to your youth group or another Christian group that includes kids who care and will reach out to him. Alert the youth leader or pastor. Encourage your friend to talk honestly to a caring adult about the way he feels. Pray for him and with him if he's open to that.

3. She needs people (in addition to her foster family) who can help fill the role of substitute family. They should be people who know God and can assure her of His presence, love, and promises. Maybe people in your church—or your own family—could do that. Some adult in the church who can act as her advocate (help her with the foster care system) would reassure her as well.

4. Tell him he can go back to school and get his high school diploma or equivalency degree—and maybe take community college classes to prepare for a career. Urge him to talk with a school counselor who can give him more information about how to get started.

5. His confusion and anger are natural; he needs to talk to a counselor, pastor, or other experienced adult about how he feels. You could suggest a person from your church. You could also help your friend "let off some steam" by playing basketball or another sport together, and by just listening.

6. She needs to tell her parents about her alcohol abuse and ask them to get her into a treatment program. If they can't do that, a counselor, physician, or pastor can direct her to one.

If you ever feel trapped, remember that your situation isn't hopeless. There are answers. And there are people who'll help you find those answers.

If time allows, close by summarizing these principles:

1. We will be pressured, but we aren't helpless.

2. God has promised a way of escape, and that way is never to "end it all."

3. Even if we fall apart at first, we can get up and trust God. He can use the experience to help us become more mature and to be a positive influence on others.

4. God's way of escape will probably mean we have to do something constructive. It may be to get away from the situation fast if that's possible, to get close to God so we'll have the strength we need, and to go for help to a mature Christian.

Most people would probably agree that it's wise to learn cardiopulmonary resuscitation (CPR) and the Heimlich maneuver in order to meet medical emergencies. But how many know how to recognize the signs that a friend is desperate and possibly suicidal? How many would know how to respond?

Those most likely to notice a teen's desperation are often friends, not professional people-helpers. Your kids need to know what to look for and how to react in ways that could save a friend's life. This session is designed to introduce them to those skills.

Throw Out the Lifeline

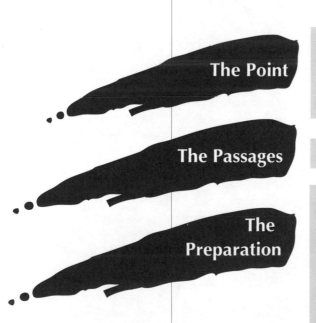

The Point

To sensitize kids to warning signs that a suicidal friend might give; to inform them of resources they can call on to help; and to show them how to reach out to a suicidal person with God's love.

The Passages

John 4:7-26; Luke 6:31; 10:27

The Preparation

You'll need the following:
• Bibles
• "Helping a Desperate Friend" (Student Sheet 27)
• Two students to read only the dialogue in John 4:7-26
• Names and numbers of the nearest crisis centers and hotlines (see your phone directory or call directory assistance)
• Chalkboard and chalk or newsprint and marker

Dial 911
Seeing the Need to Be Prepared to Give Emergency Aid

You're with a friend and the following situations happen. What will you do?

1. The friend develops a squeezing pain in his or her chest and pain in the left arm. The friend feels weak, begins to sweat, and then stops breathing. (Suspect a heart attack; call for help, begin CPR.)

2. You're eating in a restaurant and your friend chokes on a piece of food. (Do the Heimlich maneuver, expelling the food from the friend's windpipe.)

3. Your friend gets a deep cut in the forearm. He or she is losing a lot of blood. What do you do? (Apply pressure and get to the hospital.)

Do you know how to do these life-saving procedures? If kids in the group have learned, performed, or received first aid, ask a few of them to describe what happened.

If you didn't know what to do, what might happen? How would you feel?

It's important to know what to do in an emergency. It's like the Boy Scout motto. Anybody know what that is? ("Be prepared.")

Troubleshooters
Learning about Prevention and Intervention

It's not impossible that you might have to give somebody first aid. But what about intervening (stepping in to help) in the life of a desperate friend who's thinking about committing suicide? How would you feel about that? (Scared; thinking it's none of my business; not knowing what to do, etc.)

Since suicide is the second leading cause of death among people ages 15-24, it's not farfetched that someone you know might be—or become—suicidal. The person he or she would most likely talk to is a friend like you. But how can you know something's wrong? (Answers will vary, but most will boil down to listening and watching.)

In the passage we're about to hear, Jesus had stopped at a well in Samaria to rest. Let's see how he treated a person who needed help.

Before the session, line up a student to read aloud Jesus' words and another to read the woman's in John 4:7-26 (omit the rest of the narrative). Have the two read the dialogue at this point in the session.

What can we learn from Jesus about being sensitive to another person's needs? (He was tired, yet He focused on her need, not His. He knew she was an outcast because she came alone even though the well was a social gathering place. He wanted to be her Friend anyway. He knew from the questions she asked that she was looking for help.)

What things keep us from really seeing and hearing needy people around us? (Not caring; being too busy; not wanting to get involved; concentrating only on ourselves, etc.)

To help a desperate friend takes careful looking and listening. But we have to know what to look and listen for.

Warning Signals
Learning What to Look and Listen For

Distribute Student Sheet 27, "Helping a Desperate Friend." Call attention to the "Warning Signs" section and have volunteers read it aloud. Then ask the group to brainstorm specific warning signs in each category that they might observe. (A person not touching his or her food day after day in the cafeteria, cutting class, avoiding friends, defying teachers, playing with weapons, getting stoned or drunk, describing himself or herself as a failure, writing poetry or papers on a death theme, becoming cynical about God, getting involved in a Satanic cult, etc.)

Have kids read the "Lifesaver" section of the student sheet. Then form small groups and ask each to come up with and present one scenario or role play in which a student shows two of the warning signs listed. Have the rest discuss whether each situation warrants action—and if so, what to do.

What kinds of questions could you ask to get a friend to tell you how he or she feels? ("How are you?" usually gets a superficial answer; try questions like, "Do you feel sad about [an event]? I would if I'd gone through that." "You seem kind of quiet this week; is there anything you'd like to talk about?" "Has this been a good month for you?")

Write local hotline or crisis center numbers on the board or newsprint. Ask kids to copy these on Student Sheet 27.

What if the person seems suicidal but tells you to keep it a secret? To whom would you go? Read number 4 on the "Lifesaver" list; add specific names if possible.

What if you go to a person for help and he or she doesn't take you seriously?

Emphasize the fact that if the troubled person has a suicide plan, things are very serious; the person needs immediate help. Keep going to people on the list until someone agrees to take action.

If you have time, have volunteers act out a conversation between a troubled person and a concerned friend, applying principles from the student sheet.

Showing Love
Showing Concern for Troubled Acquaintances

A desperate person isn't going to change overnight. He or she needs more than one-shot concern.

Read Luke 6:31 and 10:27b, verses that encourage us to put ourselves in our friend's place. **How would you want to be treated if you were depressed enough to consider suicide?** (To be included, encouraged, built up, not abandoned, etc.)

If you were depressed and didn't know Christ, would you want to hear about Him?

Help students see that the Gospel should be shared with gentleness and sensitivity to the person's needs. Things to consider:

1. Pray for God's leading and timing.

2. Invite the person to a church activity where he or she will feel accepted.

3. Tell what Christ means to you.

4. Encourage the person to see God as loving and accepting and inter-

ested in him or her personally.

5. Don't imply that problems will go away if the person trusts God, but that He will actively help them through the dark time, day by day.

Remember, a desperate friend doesn't really want to die. He or she does want help, and you may be the one who can give it.

Close with comments like these:

It's possible that someone here is really hurting, maybe thinking about ending his or her life. Don't keep the hurt inside. Talk to me or send me a note. There is help and there is hope.

Note: Watch for students who want to talk about a desperate friend or about their own problems. Follow through as thoroughly as you can.

Read these true stories to see why the people involved were suicidal.

1. "My name is **Dave**. I'm 16 now, and life is okay. But a year ago things were different. I was so angry at my parents because I felt I couldn't please them no matter how hard I tried. Besides that, I didn't have any real friends. Drugs were easy to get, and I started using them to escape. Of course, when the drug wore off, I felt worse than ever.

"One night I grabbed a handful of pills from the medicine cabinet and gulped them down. But right afterward I began to change my mind about dying. So I got to the phone and called for help.

"With medical attention and several months of therapy, I learned how to relate better to people like my parents and the kids at school. I really believe God is the one who stopped me from killing myself. I'm so glad He did—for my own sake, and my family's, too."

2. "**Kent** was 16 years old when he took his own life. I knew him in school as shy and sensitive. He had a problem because he was different from most of the kids because of his religious beliefs. He didn't salute the flag, for example. I guess these and other things made him feel like an outsider."

3. "**Sonia** was a good friend of mine. I've been devastated since she shot herself. She was a year younger than I, outgoing, and a leader at school. But I knew she used to listen to depressing music a lot that often talked about death. Some of the things she wrote at school showed that she was troubled even though on the outside she acted okay. Some of the things she said and did showed that she was angry, too. Maybe it had to do with the fact that her parents had divorced. Maybe it had to do with trouble with her boyfriend. I'm not sure."

4. "My name is **Ben**. I was really angry all the time I was growing up. My anger got me in trouble. One reason I felt that way was because my dad died when I was very young, and my mom and I were never close. When I hit my teens, I got depressed and wouldn't go to school and slept a lot. Then I began to use alcohol. One day I had an argument with my girlfriend and I shot myself—but I lived, obviously. Since then, I've dealt with my anger and invited Christ into my life. I feel so different from the way I used to."

The Big Picture

Here are two pictures of Don's problem. The first is a close-up view. The second is a wide-angle shot. What solutions do you see in the second that you don't see in the first?

What's one problem you've faced that seemed impossible to solve—until you thought about the *"big picture"*?

A Day to Forget

Choose a word from the list that best describes how you would feel in each of the following situations. Assume that all the events take place during the same day.

Word List
annoyed
bothered
frustrated
disturbed
resentful
irritated
enraged
furious
disgusted
sad
vindictive
angry
seething
hopeless
bitter

7 a.m.
Bleary-eyed, you get dressed in your best jeans and the zipper breaks. **How you feel:**

11 a.m.
Someone hides your clothes while you're in the shower after P.E. **How you feel:**

4 p.m.
You find out that the concert you've wanted to attend for months is on the same night as your piano recital. **How you feel:**

6 p.m.
Your sister breaks a glass dish and blames you. Your mom believes her and makes you pay for it. **How you feel:**

1 a.m.
You come home after curfew because your friend really did run out of gas. When you argue loudly because your parents are suspicious, you are grounded for a week. **How you feel:**

The following is from a real account of how a teenage boy felt. Pretend he has come to you. What will you tell him?

"Nobody likes me. I have one friend—if you can call him a friend, because I know he makes fun of me behind my back. I can't be worth much if that's the only kind of person I can attract. I get so despondent, I think about ending my life. Sometimes I feel so cold inside."

List steps you think Jim should take so that he can feel life is worthwhile again.

1.

2.

3.

4.

5.

Trapped!

How would you advise the following friends?

1. "I had sex with my boyfriend because he pressured me. Now I'm pregnant and he won't have anything to do with me. I can't go to my folks. They already told me that if I ever got pregnant not to come home. I don't have anyone to turn to."

2. "Our family has moved a lot. It's hard for me to make friends in all these new places, especially because I'm small for my age and I'm not a jock. This new place is the worst ever. I'm depressed and my grades have fallen. I'll never amount to anything, unlike my brother who's six feet tall, smart, and really popular."

3. "After my dad died, my mom stayed in her room almost all the time. Finally she was put in a mental hospital. My sisters and brothers and I were split up and put in foster homes. I feel as though my life has fallen apart and I have no future."

4. "I hated school and was getting bad grades, so I dropped out. Then I got stuck in a minimum wage job and couldn't even pay my rent. So when some guys urged me to sell dope and make some quick cash, I went for it. But I got caught. Now I'm on probation. I'm worse off than before, because now I have a police record and I still can't make a decent living."

5. "My folks got divorced last year. My dad said he wanted to start a new life without a family and just walked out. I'm really mad at him for deserting us, and I feel as though maybe it's partly my fault. If I hadn't asked him for so much stuff, maybe he would have stayed."

6. "I started drinking in high school because I was very shy and it seemed to give me courage for a little while. Now I have to have a few drinks before I can face people. My folks don't know, and they want me to go to college in another state after I graduate this year. The idea scares me. I know I couldn't cope. If I can't take the pressure here, how could I ever last there? If I don't go, I'll be a disappointment to them. I feel trapped."

No Way Out?

Part I

Mark the answer you feel is true for each.

The Trap	Can Avoid	Can't Avoid
1. Getting pregnant	❑	❑
2. Addicted to drugs	❑	❑
3. Buying exam answers	❑	❑
4. Parental abuse	❑	❑
5. Dropping out of school	❑	❑
6. Chaotic home life because parents are alcoholics	❑	❑
7. Arrested for drunk driving	❑	❑
8. Keeping faith in Christ secret	❑	❑
9. Become involved in cult	❑	❑
10. Loss of friendship because you tell the truth about friends' illegal activities	❑	❑

Part II

Promise to Count On

"Watch and pray so that you will not fall into temptation. The spirit is willing, but the body is weak" (Mark 14:38).

"No temptation has seized you except what is common to man. And God is faithful; he will not let you be tempted beyond what you can bear. But when you are tempted, he will also provide a way out so that you can stand up under it" (I Corinthians 10:13).

"Because he himself [Christ] suffered when he was tempted, he is able to help those who are being tempted" (Hebrews 2:18).

I Am Not Helpless Because . . .

Helping a Desperate Friend

Know the Warning Signs

1. Changes in eating or sleeping habits, attitudes toward others, or attitudes toward school.

2. Restlessness. The person doesn't seem interested in things he or she used to enjoy.

3. Displaying feelings of hopelessness. The person has a problem and can't see any way out. He or she may seem worried, anxious, angry, guilty.

4. Taking more risks than usual—driving dangerously, for example.

5. Making statements like, "I won't be around so you won't have to worry," or, "I'm sick of living."

6. Using drugs and/or alcohol.

7. Becoming sexually promiscuous.

8. Experiencing a loss and grieving for longer than is normal.

9. Giving away things like tapes or records that are important to him or her.

10. Expressing a very low opinion of himself or herself.

11. Making suicide attempts.

12. Showing general signs of depression.

Six Ways to Be a Lifesaver

1. Take warning signs seriously. Draw out the person and try to find out more about how he or she is feeling. It's okay to ask if the person has thought of suicide; talking about it will help, not hurt.

2. If someone you know is depressed or shows two or more of the warning signs, tell a responsible adult right away.

3. If the person has plans to hurt himself or herself and confides in you, asking you not to tell, don't keep it a secret. It's better to lose a friend's confidence than a friend's life.

4. Know who to call in an emergency: a parent or other mature family member, pastor, counselor, youth leader, teacher, other school or church staff member, responsible adult friend, crisis center, or hot line. If the person has injured himself or herself, call an ambulance.

5. In a crisis situation, don't leave the person alone. Make sure there's nothing around that the person could use to hurt himself or herself; but don't put yourself in danger.

6. Don't let anyone talk you out of doing something when the situation seems to call for it. Reassure the hurting person that there's hope and that you'll get him or her together with someone who can help. Don't tell the person he or she is "stupid for talking that way." Listen; be encouraging and positive. Let the person know there are people like you who care.